BE
OUR
GUEST

BE OUR GUEST

Perfecting
the art of
customer
service

by

Foreword by
by Michael D. Eisner

EDITIONS

New York

For information, address Disney Editions, 114 Fifth Avenue,
New York, New York 10011-5690.

Library of Congress Cataloging-in-Publication Data on file.
ISBN 0-7868-5394-8

Printed in the United States of America
First paperback edition 2003
10 9 8 7 6 5 4 3 2
Visit www.**disneyeditions**.com

Always remember, the
magic begins with *you*.

TABLE OF CONTENTS

FOREWORD

by Michael D. Eisner

When you hear the name *Walt Disney Company,* it conjures up all kinds of wonderful associations—magic, creativity, wonder, imagination. Indeed, the name is so covered with Tinker Bell's pixie dust that people often just focus on the "Walt Disney" part and forget that it is still a "Company." We believe we have much in common with most other companies, the main difference being that the products we sell involve such things as flying elephants, mermaids, and lion kings.

This book details some of the effort behind the magic. For 15 years, we have offered programs on what goes into putting on the show for our guests at Walt Disney World. These programs have attracted businesspeople from an enormous range of enterprises. The response has been overwhelmingly favorable. Apparently, these businesspeople have found that we share many of the same challenges and, to be sure, we all share the same goal: satisfied customers.

We hope you will find *Be Our Guest* both interesting and useful and that it whets your appetite to learn more about what Disney Institute has to offer. As you turn the pages, we truly invite you to be our guest.

INTRODUCTION

> In this volatile business of ours, we can ill afford to rest on our laurels, even to pause in retrospect. Times and conditions change so rapidly that we must keep our aim constantly focused on the future.
>
> —WALT DISNEY

Walt Disney harnessed the talents of his "cast members" and inspired their hearts with his vision to create unparalleled entertainment experiences. He understood innately that his long-term success depended upon his ability to motivate people, one day and one innovation at a time.

The year 2001 not only commemorates the one-hundredth anniversary of Walt's birth, it also marks another important anniversary for the Walt Disney Company: the fifteenth year of providing "The Disney Approach" professional development programs to organizations worldwide. Tens of thousands of business practitioners in virtually every industry have visited Disney Institute over the years to learn more about the business behind the magic. They have found that Disney Institute programs do much more than provide a substantial learning opportunity.

These programs also inspire participants to see themselves, their organizations, and the world at large in an entirely new light.

From our earliest days, education has been a hallmark of our company. It was Walt himself who said, "We have always tried to be guided by the basic idea that, in the discovery of knowledge, there is great entertainment—as, conversely, in all good entertainment, there is always some grain of wisdom, humanity, or enlightenment to be gained." This philosophy is deeply embedded in all Disney Institute programming.

When Tom Peters and Bob Waterman profiled Walt Disney World Resort in the groundbreaking 1984 business book *In Search of Excellence* and in the companion video, corporate eyes increasingly turned to Walt Disney World Resort as a company that sets the benchmark for best business practices. To facilitate the benchmarking process, "The Disney Approach to People Management" was created in 1986.

But the corporate thirst for more information about Disney success factors could not be quenched by this one program. Over the years, others were created to highlight Disney approaches in quality service, creativity, innovation, leadership, loyalty, and supply chain excellence.

Today, Disney Institute has established a significant presence in the training world for its ability to appeal to leaders in multiple industries, and to customize content into programs that uniquely connect participants to their own heritage, values, people, and guests.

While workplace trends come and go, businesses will

always need to find new and creative ways to mobilize the brainpower, passion, and creative energies of their workforce. And that's what Disney Institute is all about.

In this book, we take you behind the scenes to discover Disney best practices and philosophies in action. We provide you with an insider's glimpse of quality service principles in action both at Walt Disney World, as told from the perspectives of cast members, and in other organizations, as told by executives who have participated in Disney Institute programs. Walt Disney's fundamentals for success still ring true. You build the best product you can. You give people effective training to support the delivery of exceptional service. You learn from your experiences. And you celebrate success. You never stop growing. You never stop believing.

We hope this book will spark new levels of performance, productivity, and pride inside your organization, by sharing some of what has made our company a legendary success over the years. This book is only a snapshot of how we make magic every day at Walt Disney World Resort. We welcome you to come and experience our programs for yourself.

We thank our editor, Wendy Lefkon of Disney Editions, for being the guiding force in making this project a reality. We thank Ted Kinni for his assistance in crafting our story. We thank our clients for sharing their stories with our readers. Most of all, we thank the many thousands of Walt Disney World cast members for their continual efforts to make a difference with guests and with each other every day.

CHAPTER 1

SERVICE, DISNEY STYLE

Kelvin Bailey was beginning to suspect that his boss might not be playing with a full deck. "We drove ten or twenty miles and we got into this nasty, wasted country," he recalls. "Water, swamps, jungle, alligators. I thought, he's got to be out of his mind—this is nothing! Water up to our knees! You couldn't have given me the land."

It was the mid-1960s. Kelvin Bailey, corporate pilot, was standing with Walt Disney in the Central Florida wilderness just southwest of Orlando, where The Walt Disney Company was in the process of buying up 30,000 acres, or 47 square miles, that would come to be known as Walt Disney World. Even though he would not live to see the park developed, Walt had no trouble seeing it amid the Florida scrub. He pointed out Main Street, Fantasyland, and other nonexistent features to the thoroughly astounded pilot.[1] But even this master of creativity couldn't have envisioned what has become the world's number-one theme park complex or, for that matter, the growth of the company that he liked to remind people "was all started by a mouse."

To be sure, Walt was capable of big dreams. Under his direction, the Disney Studios had become the world leader in the field of animated films. The first theme park, Disneyland, was the embodiment of Walt's personal vision and it was Walt who made the Disney brand synonymous with the finest in family entertainment. But even those accomplishments were simply a foundation for the company's eventual success. Walt's mouse would roar.

The Walt Disney Company is, as current Chairman and CEO Michael Eisner rightly points out, "a work in progress." If, however, you had taken a snapshot of the company at the turn of the millennium, you would have captured a portrait of the third-largest media company in the world, encompassing five major businesses: media networks, studio entertainment, theme parks and resorts, consumer products, and Internet and direct marketing.

As Eisner reported to Disney shareholders, the company has seven theme parks (with four more in the works), 27 hotels with 36,888 rooms, two cruise ships, 728 Disney stores, a broadcast network, 10 TV stations, nine international Disney channels, 42 radio stations, an Internet portal, five major Internet Web sites, and interests in nine U.S. cable networks. Moreover, in the 1990s, Disney enhanced its library with 17 animated films, 265 live-action films, 1,252 animated television episodes, and 6,505 live-action television episodes.[2]

Disney's assets have produced an enviable return on investment. Corporate revenue growth has averaged 16 percent annually since 1945 and over the past fifteen years, Disney stock has returned a 24-percent compound annual return. In fiscal 1999, revenues closed in on $24 billion, of which over $6.1 billion was generated by the Disney theme parks.

By 1996, Disney's ever-growing theme parks had been visited by more than 1.2 billion people. In 1997, there were six Disney theme parks and they ranked first through sixth in terms of worldwide global attendance, a grand slam in the industry.[3] Thanks to the insight and vision of Walt Disney, Walt Disney World Resort in Orlando, Florida, is the largest of them all.

The Walt Disney World Resort complex features four theme parks, three water parks, 27 hotels (including those owned by other companies) with more than 25,000 rooms, and almost 300 restaurants and eateries. It includes Downtown Disney, an entertainment and shopping district, Disney Institute, the complex's educational arm, and even a Wedding Pavilion (thousands of weddings have been held on the property since 1991).

This is a good-sized city located in an area about twice the size of Manhattan. Walt Disney World is the largest single-site employer in the United States and it operates every day of the week, year round. It is run by a workforce of more than 55,000 "cast members"—that's Disney-speak for employees. (To get an idea of the scale, consider that there are a half dozen physicians working at Walt Disney World who are dedicated solely to the guests.) This city can have hundreds of thousands of people in it on a crowded day. The cast itself entertains and otherwise serves millions of "guests" (that's right, Disney-speak for customers) every year. The energy that powers this city? *Magic*.

PRACTICAL MAGIC

"Magic" is not a word that is much used in the corporate world. It is not listed on the standard balance sheet (although you could say that accounting intangibles such as "goodwill" include magic). Your accounting staff is probably not measuring magic's return on investment nor is it amortizing magic over thirty years. Magic is, however, a common word in the executive suites at The Walt Disney Company.

"The magic of a Disney vacation," says Michael Eisner, "is to me the magic of quality, the magic of innovation, the magic of beauty, the magic of families coming together, the magic of our cast members. All of these things kind of bundle together."[4]

Just because you cannot assign a numeric value to magic does not mean that it is not playing a powerful role at Disney and in other companies around the world. In fact, it is easy to see the effects of magic on business, particularly at a place like Walt Disney World. Just watch the guests. Observe the toddler whose turn has come to meet Mickey Mouse, life-size and in person; the teenager who has just emerged from The Twilight Zone Tower of Terror's thirteen-story free fall; or the parents who get back to the hotel after a long day and find a Winnie the Pooh plush doll with cookies and milk patiently waiting on the bed for their child. Each is a magical moment in which the bond between customer and company is forged and strengthened. Each contributes another small boost to Walt Disney World's customer retention rate of over 70 percent.

Think for a moment about a magic show. To the audience, the show elicits feelings of wonder and surprise. Most of those watching have no idea how the magician is creating the effects they are witnessing on the stage. Not knowing how an illusion is created and simply enjoying the show are a big part of the fun. The magician's perspective is completely different. To the magician, a magic show is a highly practical task, a series of repeatable steps designed to create a fixed result and delight the audience.

The same thing happens at Walt Disney World and in all other companies that create magical customer experiences. The happy surprise that a well-served customer feels is a result of hard work on the part of the company and its employees. For the customer, the magic is a source of wonder and enjoyment. For the company and its employees, magic is a much more practical matter.

"Disney really has practical magic figured out. Not that we get it perfect every time, but we come very, very close a lot of the time," explains Michael Eisner. "You can go anywhere in the world and see that in action. Go visit Disney's Animal Kingdom in Lake Buena Vista or take one of our cruise ships to the Disney island, Castaway Cay. If you look at people's faces, you'll see that Disney still knows how to sweep people off their feet, out of their busy or stress-filled lives, and into experiences filled with wonder and excitement."[5]

For years, Disney cast members talked of "sprinkling pixie dust" to create magical experiences for their guests. But there is no line item for pixie dust on any Disney expense report. The pixie dust is the show that has been created—a show that runs at Walt Disney World from the moment guests arrive on the property until they leave for home.

In this book, as in the opening sequence of *The Wonderful World of Disney* that so many of us watched on television on the Sunday nights of our youth, we will pull back the curtain and take a look at the making of Disney's practical magic. We will explore the business behind the magic: how the company has come to set a world-class benchmark for magical service, what the main ingredients of its pixie dust really are, and most importantly, how you can create your own brand of practical magic.

MAGIC IN YOUR ORGANIZATION

Chances are very good that you are not working in a theme park such as Walt Disney World. Perhaps your company makes components for airplanes or sells business-to-business software online, or perhaps you aren't in "business" at all. You might work in a school, a hospital, or a government agency. Perhaps, at first glance, Disney's magic does not seem to have a place in your business. Perhaps it is time to broaden your perspective.

Disney Institute facilitators use a simple exercise to help guests (in this case, the hundreds of thousands of people from more than 35 countries and 40 industries who have come to Disney Institute to learn the business behind the magic) understand how similar Disney actually is to their own companies and institutions. What, they ask their classes, are the challenges your organizations are facing? The answers usually come fast and furious:

increased competition, tight labor markets, learning to partner effectively, customer satisfaction, and so on. It is a familiar list. Disney, the facilitators respond, faces the exact same challenges:

- Success breeds competition, and the competition is as hot as ever in the theme park business. One rival invested over 1 billion dollars in a park within 10 miles of Walt Disney World. The competition is not restricted to theme park operators; when executives from Harley-Davidson, Inc. attended Disney Institute, they suggested that their company was a Disney competitor because both companies vie for consumers' discretionary income.

- Walt Disney World employs 55,000 people in the Orlando area. They are working under 10 collective bargaining agreements with 32 separate unions and in 1,500 different job classifications. All are called upon to work hard.

- The need to provide guests with an ever-greater diversity of experiences has led Walt Disney World to bring new partners onto its properties. The challenge is to maintain Disney standards in restaurants and hotels the company does not own and to make passing between these separate businesses a seamless experience for guests.

- Finally, the classic service conundrum. Customer retention requires customer satisfaction, but customer satisfaction is a moving target. Consumers as a whole are more demanding than ever, and rightly so. Further, delighting the repeat guests on whom Walt Disney World depends means raising the service bar with every visit.

You have more in common with Disney than just business challenges. Underneath the trappings of our organizations, we are all driving toward the same goal—serving the people who purchase our products and services. No matter whether you call them customers, constituents, or patients, we all must satisfy our guests or risk losing them.

Even those businesses traditionally known as product companies have come to realize that they are also in the service business. There are service-based processes in every business. We take orders, create goods to suit specific needs, and deliver them according to customer instructions. Everyone has customers, and everyone needs to know how to create service magic.

Finally, as strange as this might sound, these days we are all in show business. In their recent Harvard Business School Press book, *The Experience Economy*, B. Joseph Pine II and James Gilmore suggest that we've seen the demise of the Industrial Economy, which was focused solely on the efficient production of goods, and are past the peak of the Service Economy, which wrapped products in bundles of services to make them more attractive to customers. Now, say the authors, we are entering a new age of competition that they call the Experience Economy. Goods and services are simply props to engage the customer in this new era. Customers want memorable experiences and companies must become stagers of experiences.

Pine and Gilmore make a point of describing the ephemeral nature of experiences. "However, while the *work* of the experience stager perishes upon its performance (precisely the right word), the *value* of the experience lingers in the memory of any individual who was engaged by the event," write the authors (the italics and parentheses are theirs). Sounds a lot like practical magic. They go on to use Disney as an example of a notable experience stager. "Most parents," they continue, "don't take their kids to Walt Disney World just for the event itself, but rather to make the shared experience part of the everyday family conversation for months, and even years afterward."[6]

It is easy to picture Walt Disney nodding in agreement with these ideas. As we'll discuss in more depth later, when Walt threw his energies into the creation of Disneyland in the early 1950s, he was totally concentrated on the guest experience. In fact, the very idea for Disneyland was germinated during the Sunday trips to amusement parks that Walt made with his two daughters. In those days, amusement parks were slightly disreputable and often dirty and in poor repair. While he waited for his daughters to finish their rides, the successful animator began to watch the other customers and how they reacted to the parks. He asked himself, how could this experience be improved?

Walt's answer was to create a new kind of amusement park, and since that beginning, Disneyland and all of the company's theme parks have been intensely focused on the guest experience. When you talk to Disney cast members about the parks, you will hear them described as "living movies," movies in which the guests themselves participate. As if no more elaboration was needed, Walt himself simply said, "Disneyland is a show."[7] With the infusion of some practical magic, your business could be too.

DEFINING PRACTICAL MAGIC

The Disney theme parks and their many cast members make a clear distinction between being on- and offstage. In Disney-speak, cast members are on stage whenever they are in the public areas of the parks and in front of guests. They are backstage when they are behind the scenes and out of their guests' sight in the many areas of the park where the everyday work of operating a city devoted to entertainment is conducted.

Practical magic also has its on- and offstage components. In this case, the onstage component of practical magic is the response that it produces in guests when everything comes together in a seamless, seemingly effortless performance. The backstage component is comprised of the nuts and bolts of creating practical magic. It includes all of the operations that add up to onstage magic. We are going to spend most of this book exploring that backstage component, an endlessly repeating metaprocess that Disney calls its Quality Service Cycle. To push the theater metaphor one step further, you can think of "practical magic" as the stage name for the Quality Service Cycle, the less glitzy given name for the work that produces the magic.

Before we explore the elements of this cycle and how they come together, we should be clear about what Disney means when it talks about Quality Service. Happily, it is a jargon-free, easy-to-understand definition. *Quality Service means exceeding your guests' expectations and paying attention to detail.* If this definition feels less than astounding, think about how you feel when you learn how a magic trick is accomplished. Suddenly, it all seems so simple. Like the magic show, there is no mystical incantation behind Disney's success, and anyone can learn and adapt the company's formula for practical magic. The challenge comes from living the two requirements of the Quality Service definition, and that is a lot harder than speaking them aloud.

The Wow Factor

There is one thing that every guest brings to Walt Disney World along with their families and friends—expectations, often very high expectations. Wowing guests, to borrow a word from Tom Peters, means not only meeting these preconceived notions of what a Disney vacation should be, but exceeding them. In the same way, you must first meet and then exceed the expectations of your customers, if you are going to build a reputation for Quality Service.

Many companies wow their customers, on occasion. Someone goes above and beyond the call of duty, solves a problem, and earns some high-profile gratitude from a customer. Maybe that employee will get a premium parking spot for a month or a certificate for pizza. The story will be told and retold, will perhaps be added to corporate lore— but then it's back to business as usual. That is not enough.

At the Walt Disney World Resort, exceeding guests' expectations is the standard call to duty, and if you study the resort, you can see how that works on myriad occasions each day. It shows up in a restaurant hostess's willingness to provide not only directions when you are lost but to leave her post to guide you to your destination. It appears at the end of some late-night shopping in Downtown Disney when the cashier takes the time to find out who you are and where you are staying, and then recommends the free boat ride back to the hotel and offers up a map to the dock. In Disney Institute programs, facilitators are not surprised as they listen to their guests tell stories like these each morning. "That's the cast's job," is their pithy response.

As we will see, superlative face-to-face service is just one element in the work of exceeding guest expectations. It means paying close attention to every aspect of the guest experience. It means analyzing that experience from the guest's perspective, understanding the needs and wants of the guest, and committing every element of the business—from the design of each element of the infrastructure to the interaction between guest and cast—to the creation of an exceptional experience for each of them.

Bumping the Lamp

There is corporation-wide obsession with attention to detail at Disney. Founder Walt Disney was famous for his eye for detail and he made sure that everyone paid the same attention to detail that he did.

The seeds of the company's obsession were planted during its early years when its only business was the making of animated films. Animation is a rigorous art. Twenty-four frames per second, each a still portrait of that fractional moment, must come together to create an entire story, a complete world designed and populated with characters. The ability to capture the minds and emotions of audience members is entirely dependent on the depth and consistency of the animator's vision. There is no famous actor to carry the weight, no spectacular natural setting.

Walt brought the attention to detail inherent in the animator's art to all of his company's ventures and that tradition carries through to the present day. Today, it is communicated by the catchphrase "bumping the lamp" and a story that Michael Eisner likes to tell.

"Bumping the lamp" was born during the filming of the Walt Disney Pictures film *Who Framed Roger Rabbit*. The film was an innovative mix of live action and animation. In the scene, the movie's leading man, Bob Hoskins, bumps into a lamp hanging from the ceiling. The lamp swings back and forth, and so does its shadow. During the making of the film, the lamp and its shadow appeared in the live-action setting the same way they would in the natural world. But what happened when the animated star, Roger Rabbit, was added to the scene? That's right, no shadow crossed our wisecracking hero's face.

Most of the film's viewers would not notice the difference, and certainly the scene could have been shot without Hoskins bumping into the lamp. But the film's animation artists made sure that the shading on Roger Rabbit accurately reflected the moving shadow cast by the live-action lamp in each of the 24 frames in every second of the scene. They paid attention to the details and took that extra step in their commitment to a quality guest experience.

"We start with a strong concept—the story in this case—hire the very best people to make it happen, and *bump the lamp*," says Eisner.[8]

The attention to detail at Walt Disney World is just as intense. You'll see it in the hotel room doors that have two peepholes, one at the usual height and one at a child's eye level. You'll see it also in the regular 27-foot intervals between trash cans—the park's designers figured out exactly how far an average person would carry a piece of trash before pitching it. Take a quick survey of those trash cans as you move from one area of the Magic Kingdom to another: you'll notice that their design changes to reflect each area's theme.

Exceeding guests' expectations and paying attention to detail are inextricably interwoven tasks. In tending to details, Disney consistently exceeds the expectations of the guest. Perhaps they are never consciously noticed at all—guests' attention is simply never interrupted by something that should be there, but isn't. When the experience is consistent, seamless, and of high quality, guests return. This time, they come with heightened expectations, which, in turn, incite Disney to even greater attention to detail. It adds up to Quality Service at Disney and it can add up for your organization, too.

Exceeding expectations and attending to the details are two actions you can undertake to create practical magic for your customers, but they are not, in and of themselves, sufficient to drive the day-to-day work of Quality Service. We can simply command everyone in our companies to wow customers and bump the lamp, but the results will surely leave something to be desired. There is a good chance that go-getters on your staff will take off running in opposite directions implementing their own versions of those two jobs, and the rest will shift around uneasily and finally ask, How exactly are we expected to do that?

That question, which is entirely logical, is answered with Disney's Quality Service Cycle. This is the organization-wide process that generates quality service. It is the production process through which practical magic is created. In its essence, the cycle creates a shared vision of service and then aligns the major elements that every organization shares—its people, infrastructure, and processes—in a cohesive, comprehensive effort to deliver that vision.

The body of this book is devoted to exploring how the cycle works and how it is applied within Disney and in a variety of other organizations, commercial and institutional, that have used the Disney Institute as a source of ideas and concepts for creating their own service strategies.

INTRODUCING THE QUALITY SERVICE CYCLE

At the Disney Institute, the Quality Service Cycle is composed of four main elements: a service theme, service standards, delivery systems, and integration. The cycle can be thought of as a continuous loop with customers or guests in the middle of the circle.

The Magic of Service

For Disney, the Service Cycle actually begins in the center of the loop, with the needs, wants, perceptions, and emotions of its guests.

"Guestology" is what Disney calls the art and science of knowing and understanding customers. The information that guestology provides is the basis for movement through the cycle. It helps establish an initial course of action, and as new information is gathered, it is used to fine-tune and improve performance.

The Quality Service Cycle is centered on an organization's *service theme*. A service theme is a simple statement which, when shared among all employees, becomes the driving force of service. At Disney, this theme is: *To create happiness for people of all ages everywhere*. This vision serves as a rallying flag. It aligns the efforts of cast members and establishes a foundation for their own behavior toward guests. For management, the service theme becomes a guiding precept. Every decision can be measured against it. Whether a decision supports the service theme is an important managerial litmus test.

Service standards set the criteria for actions that are necessary to accomplish the service theme and serve as the measures of quality service. There are four service standards at Walt Disney World. In order of importance, they are *safety, courtesy, show*, and *efficiency*. As we'll see later, they are ordered in strict priority, which further guides the efforts of cast members and helps facilitate decision making at the parks.

Every business will have a unique service theme and its own service standards. In chapter 2, we will find out how a service theme and standards are created and used at Disney and at a variety of other organizations, and discuss the basic tools and techniques of guestology.

With our service theme and standards in place, we move onto the delivery systems of the Quality Service Cycle. There are three delivery systems that all companies share: their employees, their setting, and their processes. Each is explored, in turn, in chapters 3, 4, and 5.

The Magic of Cast

In the past few decades, organizations everywhere have begun to understand that their employees are their most important asset. This is particularly true in the delivery of Quality Service. Often, employees are on the front lines, face-to-face with customers. And, even when they are not in direct contact with customers, they are controlling the operation of the processes by which service is delivered. The Disney theme parks have been measuring the impact of cast on the guest experience for more than forty years. What is one of the most-often stated reasons why guests return for another visit? The cast.

"Nothing so visibly defines Disney's parks as the warmth and commitment of our cast members over the years, and the appreciation that guests feel for the way they are treated," writes Michael Eisner.[10] This statement and results behind it would have surely made Walt Disney proud. After all, a friendly, approachable, and helpful cast was an important element in his vision for a new kind of amusement park from the outset.

Preparing the cast is an essential task that starts with the introduction and dissemination of a generic, organization-wide set of image and behavior standards. At Disney, every new cast member learns these *performance tips* during their first on-the-job experience, the Disney Traditions orientation program. One aspect of this training that you have already been exposed to is its language. The very words that are used to describe customers, work, employees, and so on also suggest the way that cast members will be expected to approach their roles.

As in other organizations, Walt Disney World cast members play a huge number of different roles. So, a large part of the work of equipping the cast with the information and tools they need must be conducted on the job. This requires the creation of location-specific *performance cultures*. A performance culture is a set of behaviors, mannerisms, terms, and values that are taught to new cast members as they enter their job location.

The generic performance tips that define behavior across the organization and the job-specific performance culture are both used to build the skills and talent of the cast. They also provide a baseline for evaluation and improvement.

The Magic of Setting

In Disney-speak, your setting is wherever your customers meet you. Whether that is a retail store or a hospital or a Web site or even a telephone call center, the setting that customers experience plays a critical role in how they perceive their encounter with your organization. The importance of managing the effect of setting on the guest experience can be summed up in two words: *Everything speaks.*

Here's a quick example from Disney's history. John Hench, one of the original Disney Imagineers (the folks who design and build all of the theme parks), remembers watching Walt Disney finesse a setting: "I was so astonished by the way Walt would create a kind of live-action cross-dissolve when passing from one area of Disneyland to another. He would even insist on changing the texture of the pavement at the threshold of each new land because, he said, 'You can get information about a changing environment through the soles of your feet.'"[11]

At the Walt Disney World Resort, "everything speaks" means that every detail from the doorknobs to the dining rooms sends a message to guests. The message being sent must be consistent with the service theme and standards, and must support and further the show being created. And, the next time you are in the Magic Kingdom, have some fun and pay attention to what your feet sense as you walk from one themed area to the next.

Setting includes the environment, the objects located within the environment, and the procedures that enhance the quality of the environment. We will be exploring several specific ways to work with setting in the Quality Service Cycle: we will see how setting can incorporate service standards; how it can guide the guest experience, and how it can speak to all of a guest's senses.

The Magic of Process

Processes often encompass and utilize both cast and setting, and they comprise the most prominent service delivery system in most organizations. At Walt Disney World, service processes include moving guests through the attractions, the check-in and checkout processes at the resort's hotels, and the response to emergencies, such as medical problems and fires.

There are combustion points in every process. These are spots where even a finely tuned process can break down (especially when several hundred thousand guests are straining its capacity) and instead of contributing to a positive customer experience, begin to turn a guest's good day into a bad one. It's impossible to completely eliminate combustion points, but the goal is to stop them from turning into explosion points.

One example Disney facilitators like to use involves a common parking problem. Guests very often forget where they left their car eight or ten hours before at the start of a long day of fun. The lots are labeled, the rows are numbered, and the trams that shuttle guests to the entrance announce those location devices as a reminder, but inevitably and regularly cars are misplaced.

Instead of leaving guests forlorn and wandering, members of the parking lot cast came up with a service patch. Since the parking lots are filled in order, the tram drivers started keeping a simple list of what row they were working at what time in the morning. The lists are copied and distributed to members of the parking cast at the end of the day, so if guests can remember about what time they arrived, a cast member can tell them approximately where they parked. Combustion point defused.

Debugging, as in the lost-car problem, is one of the process issues we will explore in more detail. We will also look at three other process-based issues that add quality to the guest experience: cast-to-guest communication, or how to be sure the cast can solve guest problems; guest flow, or How long is that line?; and service attention, or how to handle guests who cannot utilize a service process.

The Magic of Integration

The last element of the Quality Service Cycle is integration. Integration means quite simply that each element in the cycle is combined to create a complete operating system. Cast, setting, and process are merged in pursuit of the service theme and standards. The result: the exceptionally high-quality guest experience that drives the success of all organizations known for service excellence.

Integration is a logical, step-by-step process. You will see an easily adapted matrix as a guide to successfully achieving integration. The Integration Matrix not only serves as a battle plan for attaining Quality Service, it can also be used to troubleshoot service problems and benchmark the practices of other organizations, including Disney.

End Notes

[1] Kelvin Bailey's recollections of his trip with Walt Disney are recorded in *Remembering Walt: Favorite Memories of Walt Disney* by Amy Boothe Green and Howard Green (Disney Editions, 1999), pp. 178–179.

[2] Michael Eisner's inventory was included in his letter to shareholders in The Walt Disney Company's 1999 annual report.

[3] See Walt Disney Imagineering Vice Chairman Marty Sklar's essay in *Designing Disney's Theme Parks: The Architecture of Reassurance* (Flammarion, 1997).

[4] The quote appears in the Participant's Manual for the Disney Institute's Disney Approach to Quality Service for Healthcare Professionals seminar.

[5] See Suzy Wetlaufer's interview with Michael Eisner, "Commonsense and Conflict," in the Jan–Feb 2000 issue of *Harvard Business Review*.

[6] See *The Experience Economy* by B. Joseph Pine II and James H. Gilmore (Harvard Business School Press, 1999), pp. 11–12.

[7] The quote appears in *Walt Disney: Famous Quotes* (Disney Kingdom Editions, 1994).

[8] This story is told by Michael Eisner in a video segment of the Disney Institute's Quality Service program.

[9] Walt Disney's lifelong interest in railroads is best documented in Bob Thomas' biography, *Walt Disney: An American Original* (Hyperion, 1994). See also Richard Schickel's *The Disney Version: The Life, Times, Art, and Commerce of Walt*

Disney (Ivan R. Dee, 1997), and for young readers, Katherine and Richard Greene's *The Man Behind The Magic: The Story of Walt Disney* (Viking, 1998).

[10] See Michael Eisner's book, *Work In Progress: Risking Failure, Surviving Success* (Hyperion, 1999), p. 228.

[11] John Hench's quote appears in *Remembering Walt: Favorite Memories of Walt Disney* by Amy Boothe Green and Howard Green (Disney Editions, 1999), p. 156.

CHAPTER 2

THE MAGIC
OF SERVICE

In 1928, Mickey Mouse stormed the box office and has since become a global icon. The cartoon mouse, born of the imagination and voice of Walt Disney and the artistry of Ub Iwerks, who was the first in a long line of Disney animation masters, was not, however, an instant star. Even though Walt Disney was offering up the first cartoon with a sound track, he could not find a film distributor willing to bring the mouse to theaters.

It was a New York City theater operator and promoter named Harry Reichenbach who finally offered Walt a solution. "Those guys don't know what's good until the public tells them," said Mr. Reichenbach of the distributors. And, he convinced Walt to show *Steamboat Willie* in his theater for two weeks. It was a hit with the moviegoers and, just as he had predicted, the distributors flocked to sign up Disney and its mouse.

Walt had learned an important lesson about the power of Disney's audience. When he wanted to launch "The Skeleton Dance," the first of the studio's innovative Silly Symphony cartoons in 1929, the distributors rejected him once more. This time, they wanted "more mice." So Walt went directly to the audience, and their acceptance again powered a distribution deal. And in 1948, when he had trouble finding distribution support for *Seal Island*, the first of Disney's nature/adventure films, Walt went to the audience yet again for the help he needed. And he got it.[1]

Pick a group of people in any major urban area around the world and ask them about Walt Disney. They will invariably associate the man with the name of an animated character, a movie, or a theme park. He should be just as famous for his achievements as a guestologist. Although he was a master at knowing and understanding customers, he certainly never heard of service concepts such as "customer-focus," "close to the customer," and "customer-centric." And yet, in his straightforward, Midwestern way, Walt clearly understood that customers were the most important—and the final—judges of the entertainment produced at his company.

"We are not trying to entertain the critics," he would say. "I'll take my chances with the public."[2] But, like all the best guestologists, Walt was usually not taking much of a chance. Invariably, he had already polled the opinions of the company's customers and had included their advice in the refinement of his ideas.

Popular actor Kurt Russell, who spent his teen years making live-action movies for Disney, was surprised by the attention the head of the studio paid to him. "Sometimes he'd come down to the set and ask, 'Do you want to see a part of the movie that's being put together?' So I'd watch a movie or parts of a movie with him and we'd talk about it and he'd ask me questions," recalls Kurt. "What was interesting about Walt, as I look back on it now, is that he was picking the mind of an uninhibited thirteen-year-old. He would ask, 'What do you think of this?' and we'd kick ideas back and forth. I think he was finding out how a young mind worked."[3]

Walt's drive to find out what and how an audience thought extended into Disneyland. The next time you walk through the arched entry tunnels of Disneyland and emerge into Main Street, USA, look to your left at the Fire Station located next to City Hall. The station overlooks the Town Square. If you examine its facade, you will see a lamp burning in one of the second-story windows. The light is a tribute to Walt Disney; it illuminates the small apartment that he used as his headquarters while overseeing the construction of the park and its early days of operation. From the window of that apartment, Walt watched Disneyland's guests as they got their first impressions of the park.

Lest the image of Walt peering out above the crowd give you the idea that he was shy about face-to-face encounters with guests, nothing could be further from the truth. He not only reveled in sharing the experience of Disneyland, he made a regular practice of wandering the park collecting the responses of guests.

Tony Baxter, who eventually became a senior vice president at Walt Disney Imagineering and served as the executive designer of Disneyland Paris, had various jobs at Disneyland as a teenager, and he would bring his younger sister to the park with him. She played while he worked. One day, his sister and a friend saw Walt in the park and followed him to It's a Small World. The three of them rode through the attraction and when it was over,

Walt asked if they liked it enough to do it again. Yes, came the answer. Walt replied, "Then you need to sing the song this time" and the trio, two children and the leader of a corporate empire, took a second trip.[4]

When it was suggested that an administration building be erected for the management at Disneyland, Walt was vehemently opposed. "I don't want you guys sitting behind desks. I want you out in the park, watching what people are doing and finding out how you can make the place more enjoyable for them."[5] When he found that the staff was leaving the property to eat, Walt steamed, "Stand in line with the people and for God's sake, don't go off the lot to eat like you guys have been doing. You eat at the park and listen to people!"[6]

The most impressive result of Walt's spirited emphasis on knowing and understanding customers is Walt Disney World itself. In the late 1950s, Walt was already planning a new park somewhere in the eastern half of the United States, but he was not 100-percent sure that a Disneyland-style park would appeal to the citizens on the East Coast. The 1964 World's Fair in New York gave him the perfect opportunity to test his unique brand of entertainment using someone else's money and the biggest focus group ever assembled—the tens of millions of people who attended the fair in 1964 and 1965. Walt corralled several sponsors, and WED Enterprises, which would later become Walt Disney Imagineering, created four major attractions, including It's a Small World for Pepsi-Cola. It was estimated that 50 million people had seen at least one of the four Disney attractions, which were acclaimed as the most popular of the fair. The East Coast audience for a new Disney park was clearly established.

GUESTOLOGY REVEALED

Since guestology sounds complex and somewhat mysterious, let's pull back the curtain a bit. "Guestology" is Disney-speak for market and customer research, and, as mentioned in chapter 1, it is the work of learning who guests are and understanding what they expect when they come to visit. The time and effort that Walt Disney World devotes to guestology offers a good idea of how important it is to the ultimate success of the resort and, for that matter, any organization that undertakes the Quality Service journey.

The Walt Disney World guestology budget is invested in a whole slew of techniques, some of which your organization probably also uses. On the property, there are face-to-face surveys conducted at the park gates and other main access points. Specific "listening posts" are created as dedicated locations to answer guest questions, solve problems, and collect information. Comment cards are as common as smiles and, perhaps most important, cast members throughout the resort collect and report the opinions and observations of guests as a standard part of their jobs.

Utilization studies, too, contribute to the Walt Disney World guestology database. Usage and visitation patterns at the resort are analyzed and compared. Do guests seem to visit Pirates of the Caribbean early or late in the day? How many guests use the resort's transportation systems

Whatever we accomplished is due to the combined effort. The organization must be with you or you don't get it done. . . .
In my organization there is respect for every individual, and we all have a keen respect for the public.

—WALT DISNEY

each hour? What are the occupancy rates at the various resorts? Such studies are all part of the Quality Service brew.

Mystery shoppers make purchases to verify service in the resort's many stores and gift shops. Telephone surveys are used to develop information from both random population samples and recent guests. Guest letters and e-mails are studied for more clues to improving service. And, focus groups are used to gather information for future development and the refinement of existing rides and attractions.

A Disney Institute training client, Cherie Barnett, has made good use of focus groups in the expansion of her Michigan-based chain of hair emporiums, Glitz Salons. When an industry statistic pinpointed girls between the ages of 10 and 16 as the largest consumers of cosmetics, Ms. Barnett started thinking about a hair salon targeted directly at that niche market. The first thing she did was reach out to her potential audience.

"I got on the phone and asked them to come to my house and talk to me about this. I grabbed kids from the region—bring your friends, don't bring Mom," recalls the entrepreneur. "I worked with groups of twenty to twenty-five at a time. I asked them to tell me what they wanted in a salon, what music, decorations, logo. The ideas and how their minds worked were incredible. They actually created the logo, I just took it to the marketing people and said 'make it.'" The result was Glitz NXT, which became the third salon in the privately held chain.

Information developed by using guestology techniques is utilized in many ways. Obviously, there is no point in investing a single cent in market research if the findings are hidden away in a desk drawer. The knowledge developed from guests must be used to create and improve all the elements of the Quality Service Cycle, from the service theme and standards to the smallest detail of the service delivery systems of cast, setting, and process. The major applications of customer data are to establish a baseline and other criteria for the

You don't build it for yourself. You know what people want and you build it for them.

—WALT DISNEY

development and implementation of a service strategy and to create improvements and other adjustments to the existing service plan. Walt Disney World uses guest input for all these purposes.

Guestology surveys must be made regularly to be useful. People change and so do their expectations. Similarly, guests at Walt Disney World have changed over the years. A survey conducted among guests in 1971 when the park opened would be of use only as a historical document today. Fundamental guest demographics, such as size and composition of the average party, as well as guest attitudes and expectations have shifted and they will shift again. Guestology helps track the ever-changing guest landscape and offers the cues needed to adjust service delivery.

Customer responses change over the short term as well as the long term. Guests checking out after a week of fun will feel differently than those whose credit card statement has arrived after 30 days back at home. To create a magical service experience, Walt Disney World needs to know how guests feel across a broad spectrum of time. For these reasons, it is crucial to gather information at a variety of points during a guest's experience.

Average guests will have encounters with a cast member about 60 times during their stay. Each can be an opportunity for the cast member to learn more about guests, improve the show, and build a stronger bond between Walt Disney World and its guests. We will explore how this is accomplished in the next chapter.

KNOWING AND UNDERSTANDING GUESTS

When we say that guestology is the science of knowing and understanding customers, we are also defining the two major kinds of information developed by guest research. These are *demographic* and *psychographic*. As you will see, both are important.

Demographics

At Disney, demographic information is thought of as factual knowledge about guests. Demographics mainly describe the physical attributes of a group and often comprise quantitative data. Demographic information reveals who customers are, where they come from, how much effort they expend to get here, how much they spend, etc.

Another valuable aspect of demographics is that when you know who your guests are, you automatically know who your guests are *not*. Figuring out who is *not* doing business with you sometimes triggers huge changes in service strategy, especially if you find that you are missing a large group of potential customers.

Demographics help ensure that the Quality Service Cycle is correctly targeted. This may all seem pretty elementary, but it is surprising how often demographics open an organization's eyes to basic marketplace realities.

Psychographics

Psychographic information is the category of customer research data that helps Walt Disney World to understand its guests' mental states. Psychographics offer clues to what customers need, what they want, what preconceived notions they bring to the table, and what emotions they experience. At Disney Institute, we categorize these clues as needs, wants, stereotypes, and emotions, and we think of them as the four main points of a compass—the Guestology Compass.

Developing the four points of the Guestology Compass means generating qualitative responses from customers. This is done by asking open-ended questions, inviting opinions, and encouraging customers to speak their minds. The answers add up to a portrait of guest expectations, which in turn becomes the baseline for the work of exceeding those expectations.

Let's take a closer look at the elements of the Guestology Compass with the help of two examples, Walt Disney World and BMW Canada, Inc. BMW Canada, which has sent more than 700 of its retail center personnel to Disney Institute training, was established in 1986 as a wholly owned subsidiary of Munich–based BMW AG, and it manages a network of 32 automobile and 16 motorcycle retailers across Canada.

Needs are the easiest of the four compass points to determine. What do guests need when they come to Walt Disney World? A vacation. What do they need when they go to a BMW retail center? A car. Needs tend to be obvious, usually corresponding to the products and services you offer, but they only provide the rough outline of a psychographic profile.

Wants are less obvious. They suggest a customer's deeper purposes. Many of Walt Disney World's guests want more than a simple vacation; they also want long-lived memories of a fun-filled family experience. BMW's customer may want the status of a high-performance car. As you begin to uncover wants, the contours of the customer profile take shape.

Stereotypes are those preconceived notions that every customer has of your business or industry. Guests come to Walt Disney World expecting the cast members in the park to look a certain way. At the BMW dealership, customers will expect the technicians to look a certain way. As you identify guest stereotypes, you obtain valuable clues about their expectations. These clues help fill in the features of the guest portrait.

Finally, *emotions* are the feelings that customers experience throughout their contact with your organization. At Walt Disney World, guests are likely to have a wide range of emotions during their visit. Some are positive, such as the excitement of riding Space Mountain, and some are negative, such as impatience with long lines. At BMW, car buyers experience a similar range of emotions. They may feel proud as they drive off in their new car and remorseful when they deduct its cost from their savings account. Identifying the changing emotional state of customers completes the coloring of the profile.

The following table offers several more examples of the customer profiles developed in the guestology process. As you examine it, think about what a profile of your customers would look like.

At Walt Disney World, the process of collecting and analyzing the data required to complete the Guestology

	Needs	Wants
Walt Disney World Resort	Vacation	Happiness Lasting memories
Insurance Agency	Life insurance policy	Peace of mind
Automobile Dealer	Car	Status Freedom Reliability
Financial Institution	Bank account	Financial security Investment returns

Stereotypes	Emotions
Disney is for kids	Excitement entering
Long lines	the park
Clean	Tired feet at the end of the day
Friendly	Thrill of Space Mountain
Expensive	
Fun	
You never get your	Uncertainty of
money back	whether you're
Like a neighbor who	covered when an
is there when you	emergency occurs
need help	Relief when you're
Takes forever to get	covered
paid on a claim	
Used-car salesman	The excitement of
New-car salesman	buying a car
Luxury-car salesman	Buyer's remorse
	several days later
Marble floors	Impatience over
Wool suits and	long lines at
oxford shirts	drive-up teller
Bankers' hours	Excitement as you
Long waits at	close a loan on your
the tellers	first home

Compass goes a long way toward understanding what guests expect when they come to visit. This knowledge is used to fulfill and exceed guest expectations in every element of the Quality Service Cycle.

THE POWER OF A SERVICE THEME

"My business is making people, especially children, happy," Walt Disney said a half a century ago.[7] Although it is a simple and direct statement on the surface, Walt's quote plumbs the depths of The Walt Disney Company's service ethic. It is the basis for its mission as a business; it represents what the company stands for and why it exists. It is The Walt Disney Company's *service theme*.

In 1955, as Walt's vision of Disneyland became a reality, that theme was first made manifest as a way to introduce the new park's first employees to the basics of Disney service and to guide them in their interactions with guests. In the first Disney University orientation classes, the cast was taught: *We create happiness*. There has been an alteration or two over the years, but today's new cast members hear essentially the same message. They are taught, *We create happiness by providing the finest in entertainment for people of all ages, everywhere*.

There has been a great deal of talk about organizational vision, mission, and values in the past decade. Management thinkers have identified these statements of organizational intent as highly effective workplace unifiers and have shown in studies that companies with well-defined ideologies are successful in the long term.

Jim Collins and Jerry Porras, the authors of *Built to Last,* call them Visionary Companies, and found that they "outperformed the general stock market by a factor of 12 since 1925."

"Leaders die, products become obsolete, markets change, new technologies emerge, and management fads come and go, but core ideology in a great company endures as a source of guidance and inspiration," they wrote in the *Harvard Business Review.*[8]

Many organizations got the message and quickly created statements regarding their purpose and values. They engraved them on plaques and hung them for everyone, customers and employees, to see. And, in many cases, that was about as far as the effort went; a well-chosen sentiment to which no one paid much attention. Collins and Porras say that this is because the core ideology (the purpose and values of an organization) is not something that can be simply declared. Instead, it must either reflect existing truths about a company or create new ideals that will be pursued until they become inherent truths.

Like the core purpose of companies such as Johnson & Johnson, 3M, and Hewlett-Packard, Disney's service theme is successful because it is deeply rooted in its heritage and supported throughout the day-to-day operations of the business. It is a *living* theme, not just a sentence on a plaque, and it serves three critical needs: it clearly defines the organization's purpose; it communicates a message internally; and it creates an image of the organization.

Loud and clear, The Walt Disney Company's service theme declares a mission *(to create happiness)*, how that mission is accomplished *(by providing the finest in entertainment)*, and for whom *(people of all ages, everywhere)*. Today, "entertainment" at Disney means television, films, books, theme parks, cruises, etc. But at the same time, it creates a clear focus. You will probably never see a Disney-made jet or get a home loan at the Bank of Disney. The service theme defines the purpose of an organization.

The service theme also communicates the purpose throughout the organization. It relates an ultimate goal to every one of the 120,000 people who work at The Walt Disney Company worldwide and serves as a rallying point across the organization. It is one thing that all employees have in common and no matter what the individual job, it defines the expectation that all will help create happiness for the customer.

Finally, the service theme creates the foundation for the public image of the company. It tells the guests what they can expect to get from the company (the finest in entertainment). It is an explicit promise and a double-edged sword: if guests' expectations are met or exceeded, then they are happy. If not, their displeasure will be obvious.

Even if the words sound similar, every organization creates its own unique service theme. Obviously, the Walt Disney World theme of creating happiness cannot simply be adopted and imitated: it is critical to create your own service theme. It is the fundamental element of the Quality Service Cycle.

Here's what Tom Peters and Bob Waterman had to say on the subject in their groundbreaking book,

In Search of Excellence: "Whether or not they are as fanatic in their service obsession as Frito, IBM, or Disney, the excellent companies all seem to have very powerful service themes that pervade the institutions. In fact, one of our most significant conclusions about the excellent companies is that, *whether their basic business is metal-bending, high technology, or hamburgers, they have all defined themselves as service businesses.*"[9]

The United States government spent most of the 1990s and is still today in the process of redefining itself as a service business. One of the principle tenets of the reinventing government initiative requires reorganizing governmental agencies as performance-based organizations (PBOs) that are customer-centric. The first officially mandated PBO was Student Financial Assistance at the U.S. Department of Education (SFA, for short). The SFA, a Disney Institute client, processes more than $60 billion in grants, student loans, and work-study assistance each year. Its service theme is simple and compelling: *We help put America through school.*

With that short sentence SFA directly targets its end customers, the more than 9 million American students that it helps to pursue a higher education annually. It is a critical focus because the agency does not always deal directly with the American families that need student loans. Instead, it works with partners—the schools, banks, and loan guarantors—who act as the delivery system to the ultimate customer, the student. The refocusing of attention on students was what COO Greg Woods, the leader of the reinvention effort, was talking about when he said, "We are gonna show 'em service like they've never seen, and we'll have fun doing it."[10]

It is worth noting that the first place the SFA went to learn how to better serve customers was to its customers. Mr. Woods formed a task force comprised of line personnel and they conducted 200 listening sessions with students and their parents and operating partners from around the nation. More than 8,000 customer comments were collected and analyzed *before* improvements were determined. That's guestology in practice.

Another Disney Institute client, Pick 'n Pay, the largest food retailer in South Africa, with a fiscal 2000 market share of 39 percent and more than 450 owned and franchised stores, created its own inspirational service mission. In response to the unique political, social, and business transformations in its home country, CEO Sean Summers spearheaded a project named *Vuselela,* a Xhosa/Zulu term meaning "rebirth." "We had to create a society within Pick 'n Pay that mirrored what South Africa was trying to become," the CEO told us.

The company looked to its 27,000 employees to create a mission with meaning. "We decided to tap into the heartland of the organization—the packers, the cashiers, the cleaners, the clerks, everyone—to find out what they felt the company represented," said Mr. Summers. The new service mission they articulated echoed the new society: *We serve. With our hearts, we create a great place to be. With our minds, we create an excellent place to shop.*

The Evolution of the Disney Service Theme

Year	Service Theme	Meaning
1955	We create happiness.	At the outset of the idea of the theme parks, working from the film medium heritage, happiness was identified as the "want" the guests were in search of. The "we" was the cast members, as a team.
1971	We create happiness by providing the finest in family entertainment.	The introduction of the word "finest" acknowledged that there was a marketplace and competition in turbulent times.
1990	We create happiness by providing the finest in entertainment for people of all ages, everywhere.	By the nineties, Disney had recognized the huge diversity of the potential guest population, in what was becoming a world market.
2001—and beyond	We create happiness . . .	Disney continues to monitor the changes and requirements of the guests. Even though the service theme continues to evolve, it, in some measure, remains the same.

A final note about service themes: They need not be forever fixed. After all, nothing lasts forever. But, if a service theme is properly established, it should change only very slowly, evolving over a long period of time. Collins and Porras suggest that, unlike a business strategy or goals, an organization's core purpose should last at least a century.

"Whereas you might achieve a goal or complete a strategy, you cannot fulfill a purpose; it is like a guiding star on the horizon—forever pursued but never reached," they explain. "Yet although purpose itself does not change, it does inspire change. The very fact that purpose can never be fully realized means that an organization can never stop stimulating change and progress."[11] That is as good a summation of the power of a service theme as you will find anywhere.

DEFINING THE SERVICE THEME PROMISE

Since a service theme acts as a promise to your customers and a purpose for your employees, the next logical question is: How will you fulfill that promise and purpose? The answer is the establishment of *service standards*. Service standards, or service values, are the operational criteria that ensure the consistent delivery of the service theme. They flow from the service theme and in turn, support the achievement of the theme.

At Walt Disney World, the service standards, like the service theme, are deeply rooted in the history of the company's attractions business. In the 1940s, when Walt Disney first imagined Disneyland, they were an implicit part of his vision of an amusement park that would be wholly unlike the ones he had been taking his children to visit. Walt's park would be clean, its employees would be friendly, and every member of a family could have fun in it. In 1955, when training consultant Van France and Dick Nunis, who later became Chairman of Walt Disney Attractions, created the orientation class for Disneyland's first employees, they worked from the "creating happiness" theme and started linking its achievement to specific behaviors. And, in 1962, when Dick refined those behaviors into the four components of a "good show," the park's service standards were explicitly defined.

Dick's four elements were Safety, Courtesy, Show, and Capacity (which was later relabeled Efficiency) and today, they are also Walt Disney World's service standards. They represent how the service theme is fulfilled and offer a set of filters that help Disney employees to judge and prioritize the actions that contribute to the guest experience. Let's take a closer look at the Walt Disney World service standards to see how they support the service theme:

Safety

It is a gross understatement to say that a guest who is exposed to injury or who feels insecure about his or her safety or the safety of loved ones is going to be unhappy. So, the service standard of safety requires that the welfare and peace of mind of guests are always provided for.

Imagineer Bruce Johnson explains what that means in the creation of attractions: "The statistics are very much against us. Think about it. If there is a one in a million chance something will go wrong and ten million guests ride our ride, then something will happen ten times. We can't design to that one in a million. We have to design to one in hundreds of millions."[12]

By adopting safety as a service standard, Disney ensures that safety concerns are addressed in every element of the Disney resorts and parks. Safety features, often above and beyond local codes, are designed into the resort's attractions, transport systems, hotels, and eateries. In addition to a large dedicated security staff, the entire cast resort-wide is taught safety procedures and location-specific safety practices.

Courtesy

The service standard of courtesy requires that every guest be treated like a VIP—a very important, very individual person. Fulfilling the standard means more than simply treating people the way we would want to be treated; it means treating them the way that *they* want to be treated, with recognition and respect for their emotions, abilities, and cultures.

If you live in Orlando, Florida, all you have to do is ask for directions to figure out if someone works at Walt Disney World. If the person assisting you points using two or more fingers or an open hand, odds are high that they work at the Mouse's House. That's because pointing with one finger is considered impolite in some cultures, so one of the first things all new cast members are taught is how to point courteously.

Making courtesy a service standard means turning it into a set of organization-wide behaviors. As an organization, it makes Walt Disney World responsible for recruiting, hiring, and training a cast with great interpersonal skills. The cast is taught to take a wide responsibility for guest happiness, by being friendly, knowing the answers to common questions, and, when possible, personally guiding guests to their destinations. For cast members, it means taking a proactive approach to courtesy by anticipating and reaching out to assist and engage Walt Disney World's guests. As Disney Institute facilitators say, "Guests may not always be right, but they are always our guests."

Show

The service standard of show requires that there be seamless and exceptional entertainment for guests. The service theme calls for the "finest in entertainment" and at its highest level, that means a performance that is uninterrupted from the beginning to the end of a guest's stay at the resort. The fact that the Disney theme parks are the most popular in the world is a testament to the pursuit of the standard of show.

Walt Disney was always focused on providing a good show, one in which the audience's attention was never unintentionally diverted or otherwise interrupted. Marty

Sklar, Chairman of Walt Disney Imagineering, remembers walking through Disneyland with Walt. As they reached the Mike Fink Keel Boats in Frontierland, a company publicist drove up to the pair. Walt was shocked. "What," he demanded, "are you doing with a car here in 1860?"[13]

The pursuit of a seamless show is a driving force within the organization. Story is a concept that is repeated over and over throughout Walt Disney World. Each resort is built around a story and every design detail, from the landscape to the doorknobs, supports the theme of that story. Each park is built around one or more stories and their design, from the trash containers to the refreshments, also echo their stories. From the theater language spoken to the personal appearance of cast members, the human resources of the business are an integral part of the show. Jobs are performances; uniforms are costumes. It all adds up to a seamless show.

Efficiency

The service standard of efficiency requires smooth operation of the theme parks and resorts. In doing so, guests have the opportunity to enjoy as much of Walt Disney World as they wish. Disney's profits directly correspond to the company's ability to maximize the guests' usage of the property.

The Mark VI Monorails, for example, transport more than 110,000 guests each day with a reliability rate of 99.9-percent. Since 1971, they have run safely and efficiently for more than 4 million miles.[14] Disney-designed Omnimovers keep the lines moving by carrying 2,500 guests per hour through the resort's attractions.[15]

Walt Disney World pursues operational efficiency throughout its properties. The company studies guest flow and usage patterns to provide the proper equipment and staffing levels. Operational checklists ensure preparedness for the demands of each business day. Sales levels are analyzed to provide the proper mix and quantity of products and services, establishing the optimum speed of service to ensure the best guest experience. Operational efficiency is the fourth and final driver in the achievement of the service theme.

It is, however, not enough to simply identify service standards, they must also be prioritized. Otherwise, what happens when a conflict between standards arises? Consider this: What should a cast member do when a guest using a walker enters a moving loading platform that governs the speed of an entire attraction? Does the cast member slow or stop the ride and inconvenience the rest of the riders or does she leave the guest who does not fit the mold to fend for himself?

Walt Disney World has prioritized its standards, and we have just explored them in their proper order (safety, courtesy, show, and efficiency). Once you know these priorities, the solution to the problem becomes clear. The cast member immediately knows to put the safety of a guest with disabilities ahead of the efficiency of the loading process, the continuity of the show, and even the courteous treatment of another guest. Prioritized service standards act as the guiding signals in the service theme cycle.

Finally, like your service theme, your organization's service standards will surely be different from the standards at Walt Disney World. Nevertheless, they are the deliverables of the service theme and they define and specify the criteria by which your service decisions will be made and judged.

Witness the experience of Disney Institute client Lehigh Valley Hospital & Health Network (LVHHN), a healthcare network anchored by three hospitals with 1,200 physicians and more than 6,000 employees located in Eastern Pennsylvania. LVHHN decided to break away from the stereotypical image that people have formed about healthcare organizations and adopted *All hospitals are not alike* as its service theme. The organization also developed a service promise, a commitment that each employee made: "I promise to listen, understand, and respond with the highest standards of healthcare, service, and personal respect."

The 101-year-old organization further pursued its goal by establishing five service standards that are designed to communicate the operational behaviors required to achieve the service theme and promise. These are summed up in an acronym: PRIDE. PRIDE at LVHHN stands for Privacy, Respect, Involvement, Dignity, and Empathy. Here's how the regional healthcare network defines what each standard means (as you read them notice how often they directly reflect patient concerns and needs):

Privacy: LVHHN recognizes the right to privacy and pledges to keep confidential all personal and medical information, unless it is required for diagnosis or treatment, or by the law.

Respect: LVHHN values each person's uniqueness, beliefs, rights, and needs. We are creating an environment built on concern, patience, and personal regard for everyone.

Involvement: LVHHN believes that active participation and effective communication are clearly linked to customer satisfaction. We will strive to provide timely, accurate, and complete information to others when it affects them.

Dignity: LVHHN staff members will maintain a high standard of professional conduct when representing the network. Our attitudes, actions, and words reflect our self-esteem and concern for others.

Empathy: LVHHN staff will strive to understand the unique perspective and situations of all individuals with whom they interact, including patients and their families, coworkers, physicians, and other customers.

Interestingly, the explanations of each standard were established by a group of 50 of LVHHN's best-performing employees. They were split into five groups and asked to define what each standard would look like in practice. PRIDE is a simple, memorable device for communicating service standards. Moreover, it establishes the service deliverables that the employees at LVHHN are using to make their facilities unlike those of any other hospital.

DELIVERING ON THE PROMISE

With a service theme and standards to guide us, it is time to start exploring the delivery of Quality Service. At Walt Disney World, there are three major service delivery systems. Delivery systems are the methods by which Quality Service is implemented; they are *cast, setting,* and *process.*

Cast is, of course, the employees who work in your organization. If you think for a moment about organizations known for world-class service, their employees always come to mind as a key source of service delivery. *Setting* is Disney-speak for the physical resources of your organization. It is where your customers meet you. If you have ever decided to leave a restaurant before you were even seated because of how it looked or smelled, you already know how important setting is to service delivery. *Process* represents the various series of operations that are used to deliver your products and services to customers. The late W. Edwards Deming, perhaps the most famous quality guru of all, pinpointed process as the primary determinant of product quality, and it plays just as large a role as cast or setting in the delivery of Quality Service.

The next three chapters detail how these three systems are used to deliver the service theme and standards at Walt Disney World, how they work in other organizations, and how they can work in your company.

Quality Service Cues

Become an expert Guestologist: Guestology is the work of learning who your customers are and understanding what they expect when they come to you. Guestology techniques include surveys, listening posts, focus groups, utilization studies, and most important, the feedback customers give to employees.

Create a Guest Profile: Knowledge about customers includes demographics (information about the physical characteristics of your customer base), and psychographics (information about their attitudes, lifestyles, values, and opinions). Both provide useful information for creating service quality.

Use the Guestology Compass to manage customer information: The compass collects and analyzes customer needs, wants, stereotypes, and emotions.

Articulate a unique Service Theme: A service theme defines an organization's purpose, communicates a message internally, and creates an image of the organization. At Walt Disney World: "We create happiness by providing the finest in entertainment for people of all ages, everywhere."

Define your critical Service Standards: Service standards are the criteria by which Quality Service is judged, prioritized, and measured. The four Walt Disney World service standards: Safety, Courtesy, Show, and Efficiency.

Recognize the primary Service Delivery Systems: Delivery systems are the methods by which Quality Service is implemented. Organizations have three major delivery systems: Cast, Setting, and Process.

End Notes

[1] For more detail on the role of audience see Bob Thomas' *Walt Disney: An American Original* (Hyperion, 1994).

[2] The quote appears in *Walt Disney: Famous Quotes* (Disney Kingdom Editions, 1994), p. 9.

[3] Kurt Russell's quote appears in *Remembering Walt: Favorite Memories of Walt Disney* (Disney Editions, 1999), p. 45.

[4] Tony Baxter relates this story in his interview with Didier Ghez in issue no. 22 of *"E" Ticket Magazine*.

[5] See Bob Thomas' *Walt Disney: An American Original*, p. 263.

[6] See *Remembering Walt: Favorite Memories of Walt Disney* (Disney Editions, 1999), p. 166.

[7] See *Walt Disney: Famous Quotes* (Disney Kingdom Editions, 1994), p. 21.

[8] The statistic and quote appear in James Collins and Jerry Porras' article "Building Your Company's Vision" in *Harvard Business Review*, Sept.–Oct. 1996.

[9] The italics are Thomas Peters and Robert Waterman's. The quote appears on p. 168 of *In Search of Excellence: Lessons from America's Best-Run Companies* (Warner Books, 1984).

[10] The quote comes from Greg Wood's speech at the swearing-in ceremony, Dec. 8, 1998.

[11] Collins and Porras' "Building Your Company's Vision" in *Harvard Business Review*, Sept.–Oct. 1996.

[12] Bruce Johnson's quote appears on p. 113 of *Walt Disney Imagineering: A Behind the Dreams Look at Making the Magic Real* (Hyperion, 1996).

[13] Marty Sklar's memory appears in Beth Dunlop's *Building a Dream: The Art of Disney Architecture* (Abrams, 1996), p. 14.

[14] *Walt Disney Imagineering*, p. 117.

[15] *Ibid.*, p. 115.

CHAPTER 3

THE MAGIC OF THE CAST

It only takes a quick stroll down the business aisle of your local bookstore to confirm that there are countless texts devoted to the power and ability of employees and the indispensable role they play in the achievement of organizational goals. In fact, the vital need for a fast-thinking, motivated workforce seems so logical and commonplace that it is hard to imagine that our beliefs about people at work were ever any different. But, in the 1930s, employees did not hold as respected a place in the organizational scheme as they do today.

Even Henry Ford, who in 1914 had outraged capitalists everywhere when he nearly doubled plant employees' wages to $5 a day, and in his 1922 autobiography wrote glowingly of the capacity of the American worker, had soured on the merits of the workforce by the 1930s. "The average man won't really do a day's work unless he is caught and cannot get out of it," said the inventor of the moving assembly line in a 1931 interview. He backed up this mean-spirited declaration with the force of the Ford Service Department, a group of strong-arm supervisors and security guards that, under the direction of Harry

Bennett, intimidated and physically attacked Ford laborers who did not toe the company line.[1]

In stark contrast to the mechanistic gray of Henry Ford's beliefs about employees, Walt Disney's vision was awash in color and energy. As the roaring twenties gave way to the depressing thirties, the financial and critical success of the company's first Technicolor cartoons and Walt's dream of creating the first feature-length animated movies were driving growth at Disney's Hyperion Avenue studios in Burbank, California. Walt knew that the key to the studio's continued prosperity was its workforce. So, he began an expansion plan that enlarged his six-person staff to more than 750 people and started thinking seriously about training and development.

If you were a young animator at The Disney Company in 1931 and you didn't own a car, there is a good chance that several nights a week Walt himself chauffeured you and a group of your colleagues to Los Angeles for company-paid classes at the Chouinard Art Institute. In late 1932, as attendance at these classes expanded, Walt quit driving and hired Don Graham of Chouinard to teach at the studio. "I decided to step out of their class," Walt quipped, comparing his company to the competition, "by setting up my own training school."[2] Accordingly, on November 15, 1932, the first session of the Disney Art School was held with 25 students. Attendance grew quickly, particularly after word spread about the nude models Don had posing in the life drawing class.

By 1934, the in-house school was running on a full-time basis. Newly hired animators were taught drawing in classes held at local zoos and learned production techniques in studio classes. Early in 1935, Walt analyzed the characteristics of a good animator to guide Don in the development of "a very systematic training course for our young animators . . . and a plan of approach for our older animators."[3] Soon, outside lecturers were appearing and Disney animators were learning from distinguished speakers such as architect Frank Lloyd Wright and drama critic Alexander Woollcott.

At the same time the company's first training programs were being established, Walt was formalizing the major elements of the corporate culture. Hard work and creativity were rewarded with bonus checks. The use of first names and casual dress contributed to an open atmosphere. Uninhibited story sessions, sometimes held after work in Walt's home, added a democratic element to a system based on adopting the very best ideas, no matter where they originated.

The first big payoff for all of the company's training and development efforts came on December 21, 1937, when *Snow White and the Seven Dwarfs* premiered in Hollywood to a standing ovation from the industry's elite. Composed of 2 million drawings, the critically acclaimed 83-minute feature film broke attendance records at New York's Radio City Music Hall and won a specially made Oscar that featured one regular-size statue accompanied by seven dwarf Oscars. Within six months, the receipts from the film had paid off all of the company's bank loans and, in its first run, *Snow White* earned $8 million. This was "a phenomenal sum," according to Disney biographer Bob Thomas, "considering that the average price for a theater admission in the

United States in 1938 was twenty-three cents—and a heavy percentage of those seeing *Snow White* were children admitted for a dime."[4]

Walt made a similar investment in training and development in the mid-1950s at Disneyland. In 1955, he created Disney University, the first corporate university, to make sure that new employees understood and delivered the service he envisioned at the unique new park. And in 1971, five years after Walt's death, when Walt Disney World opened in Florida, a new branch of the University was established along with it. By then, there was no debate about the investment. Everyone knew Walt had been right when he said, "You can dream, create, design, and build the most wonderful place in the world . . . but it requires people to make the dream a reality."[5]

In the Quality Service Cycle, the workforce, or the cast, is a critical delivery system of both the service theme and service standards. At the Disney parks and resorts, guests come into contact with cast over 2.5 billion times per year. Each contact, said Michael Eisner in a speech at Rutgers University, "is a chance to win over a customer or lose one." That's why, Eisner continued, "we try to make our cast members feel they are part of a family . . . that they share a special heritage . . . that a frown, indifference, or a discarded gum wrapper is an intrusion in the magic world that our theme parks are designed to create."[6]

CASTING THE FIRST IMPRESSION

It has been said before and it is worth repeating: You never get a second chance to make a first impression. At

Walt Disney World, all of the cast members know about the importance of first impressions. They understand that guests will form a first impression in seconds and how important it is to make that impression a positive one. First impressions are strong and lasting ones. But customers aren't the only people who get fast and firm first impressions, so do employees.

Before we start exploring the role of cast in service delivery at Walt Disney World, take a moment to think about what most new employees experience when they arrive for their first day of work. What was the first thing you did on your first day on the job? It was probably some kind of orientation. In *Training* magazine's 1999 Industry Report, 92 percent of respondents said that their organization offers a formal new employee orientation program. It is the most common kind of training offered.[7]

Here's one more question: What is the first impression that most new employees get on that first day at work? Well, the almost one in ten who don't participate in an orientation program don't get much of an impression at all, at least not one that their new employer has much control over. They just go to work and get to work. Even those new hires who do get an orientation are mostly treated like parts in a machine. They are imprinted with varying degrees of information that usually involve an official welcome, statements of the organizational mission and values, explanations of benefits and policies, paperwork processing, and perhaps, a code of ethics along with a menu of the penalties that code violators might expect. A few hours later, they are marching off to their new jobs and their employers have missed a golden opportunity to begin creating a workforce capable of delivering world-class service.

At Walt Disney World over the next few years, Disney will hire thousands of people annually. The Casting Center handles 150 to 200 applicants each day and about 100 jobs, including transfers and promotions, are filled daily. Prior to 1989, casting was conducted in an *ad hoc* series of offices and trailers. But in 1989, when today's center was opened, the ability to make a memorable first impression on prospective and new cast members was greatly improved.

The Walt Disney World Casting Center was designed by architect Robert A. M. Stern, who immediately understood the power that the finished building would have to impress new hires. To the new cast member, the Casting Center, he explained, "may be the only time you experience the total identity of the corporation. It's very important symbolically." Accordingly, he created an entry point to the organization that is at once elegant and playful, one that architecture critic Beth Dunlop described as "otherworldly and fanciful, as if it had dropped from the pages of a picture book; a stop frame in an animated film."

Impression-making is an integral part of the design. As prospective cast members enter the building, they grasp doorknobs patterned after the talking doorknobs in Disney's film *Alice in Wonderland.* The receptionist's desk is on the second floor at the back of the building. As you travel toward it on your own trip down a rabbit hole, you get a symbolic tour of the company through hallways and rotundas of ever-changing shapes and perspectives. Gilded figures of cartoon characters sit atop columns, scenes from Disney animated films are painted on the walls and ceilings, and the waiting room features a model of Cinderella Castle surrounded by free-form seating. "Bob [Stern] was adamant that you enter on the ground floor, and the first time you can ask for a job is at the other end of a hall on the second floor," explained Disney project director Tim Johnson. "He said, 'Let them wander. Let them get a taste for Disney before they get there.'"[8]

Picture yourself walking through this strange and wonderful building dedicated solely to the casting process. What kind of message does the fact that Walt Disney World invested so much effort in its design and materials say about how the company values its cast and particularly, how it will expect its cast members to behave? What kind of messages does your employment setting send to job applicants and new hires?

We introduced South Africa's leading supermarket chain Pick 'n Pay and its service theme in chapter 2. In addition to its inspirational theme, Pick 'n Pay is also a fine example of an organization that is investing in the creation of exceptional casting facilities. After initial visits to the Disney Institute, Pick 'n Pay began designing and building its version of the ideal supermarket. Located in the town of Guateng, the Pick 'n Pay store at Fourways Crossing was developed as a training store, where new and world-class practices could be introduced that would set a benchmark for the rest of the company.

The 121-member staff at Fourways Crossing was handpicked from applications submitted by employees across the company. In November 1998 they all came to Lake Buena Vista, along with CEO Sean Summers, for

Quality Service training at the Disney Institute. Struck by the employee-empowering capabilities of the Casting Center and Disney University, Mr. Summers altered the Fourways Crossing store design to include a corporate university.

"Building on the already planned Fourways store was at an advanced stage," general manager Danie Boshoff remembers, "but frantic transatlantic phone calls brought building to a grinding halt while plans for the store were radically altered to embody what we had learned at Disney and Disney Institute—a seamless experience from a world-class shop floor to world-class staff facilities. Why not our own Pick 'n Pay Institute where all Pick 'n Pay people would have the opportunity to learn about and experience world-class service excellence?"[9] In November 1998, the Fourways Crossing store opened along with the Pick 'n Pay Institute of Leadership and Quality Service, the first of its kind in South Africa.

OUTFITTING THE CAST FOR SERVICE DELIVERY

You might think that Walt Disney World pays a premium for extra-courteous and friendly employees or that cast members are really Audio-Animatronic figures manufactured using some secret formula cooked up by the Disney Imagineers. In fact, cast members are hired from the same labor pool as every other organization uses and are paid the going rates. The not-so-secret method by which ordinary people are transformed into Walt Disney World cast members can be found in the way they are trained.

After a successful audition (yes, Disney-speak for a job interview) for a role, the first thing that new cast members do is begin learning how to deliver Walt Disney World's brand of Quality Service. Walt Disney World uses a two-tiered approach to preparing the cast for service delivery. The first tier is conducted at Disney University and teaches concepts and behaviors that are common to every cast member throughout the organization. The second tier, which we will explore later in the chapter, occurs on the job and encompasses the location-specific information that is needed to perform in the different business units of the resort.

All newly hired cast members start their tenure at Disney with Traditions, a one-day orientation program taught by Disney University, the internal training arm of the company. The average class size is 45 people and there are about nine classes each week, with as many as 14 classes per week in peak hiring seasons. Traditions offers plenty of relevant and practical knowledge, and existing cast members serve in the role of training facilitators. Each year, a voluntary casting call is made for about 40 Traditions Assistants. It is considered an honor to perform in Traditions. Each year, those cast members who are chosen leave their daily jobs at regular intervals to teach the course. (By the way, the extra depth of knowledge and refresher training acquired by the Traditions Assistants in the course of facilitating the program is an added benefit of using veteran employees to deliver training.)

The goal of Traditions is well stated by a veteran Disney Institute facilitator who says, "We don't put people in Disney. We put Disney in people."[10] Toward that end, the program utilizes a variety of training techniques, including lecture, storytelling, video, exercises, large and small group discussion, and field experiences. Traditions is designed to accomplish four major purposes:

- To acclimate new cast members to the foundations of the resort's culture.
- To perpetuate the language and symbols, heritage and traditions, quality standards, values, and traits and behaviors of Walt Disney World.
- To create a sense of excitement about working at the resort.
- To introduce new cast members to the core safety regulations.

We have already briefly mentioned Traditions' role as the initial communicator of service theme and standards, but it does much more than that. It explains how the service theme and standards are put into practice in the resort. It is an introductory course in Disney showmanship.

Traditions, for example, explains why the cast's appearance must reflect the setting and story when they are entertaining guests. The Disney theme parks have often been complimented on, and criticized for, their strict guidelines regarding the personal appearance of cast members. While some observers have tried to politicize the issue, policies regarding hair, jewelry, cosmetics, etc. are in place for sound business reasons. They are directly and clearly related to the service standard of Show.

For a policy like this to be fair to employees and legal, it must be consistently interpreted and applied. Disney cast members are informed of appearance guidelines throughout the employment process and without exception arc not allowed to participate in the Traditions class and thus start work until their personal appearance is in compliance. That is also why changes in policy are not undertaken lightly. When Walt Disney World recently amended its guidelines to allow mustaches, for example, what appeared on the surface a simple decision actually required much internal thought and discussion. Neither employees nor the legal system will look kindly on a return to a stricter policy once it has been eased.

Disney-Speak

ATTRACTIONS: rides or shows
CAST MEMBER: employee
GUEST: customer
ONSTAGE: guest areas
BACKSTAGE: behind the scenes
COSTUME: uniform
AUDITION: interview
ROLE: job
HOST/HOSTESS: Frontline employee

Traditions also extends the mission of creating happiness through entertainment into the very language that cast members speak. You have already been exposed to the show-based vocabulary used at Disney; Traditions is where cast members learn it.

At first glance, the language may seem contrived and largely inconsequential. But words create images and corresponding assumptions in people's minds. Take the word *guest*. An unhappy guest and an unhappy consumer are likely to create two different images in an employee's mind. Guests are welcome; consumers are statistics. If someone is your guest, don't you feel a greater obligation to ensure his or her happiness? The word *performance* also creates a singular image. If you are performing in a show, are you likely to be operating at a higher level than when you are bussing tables at a restaurant? How we talk about work does make a difference.

Don't underestimate the power of a good orientation program to create a portrait of the organization and its culture in the minds of new employees. While the history, mission, and values of your business may be as familiar as a favorite childhood story to you, new employees have not yet heard them. When St. Louis–based Dierbergs, Inc., a chain of 18 supermarkets employing 4,500 people, decided to revamp its new employee orientation process, it studied how the Walt Disney World program communicated heritage and culture. "We were doing a traditional rules-and-regulations thing," recalls Fred Martels, then Dierbergs' senior human resources executive and now head of People Solutions Strategies, a consulting firm. "We told people what they could and couldn't do and what would get them fired. But that doesn't motivate people. We needed to speak to their hearts, not just their brains."

To accomplish that goal, the company created a new program that emphasized its 150-year history, the four generations of family management, and its heritage and culture of Quality Service. The orientation includes pictures from the company's history and stories of great customer service. Instead of spending all their time on company policy, a handbook of rules is given to employees. They are asked to read it after the class and return a signed statement agreeing to abide by the rules.

North Carolina–based Montreat College designed its first orientation program after its administrators visited Disney Institute for a program cosponsored by Washington, D.C.'s Council of Independent Colleges, a national association of more than 480 private liberal arts institutions. Montreat College, a Presbyterian not-for-profit with six satellite campuses and about 1,100 students and 300 staff members, appears to grow out of the mountains of western North Carolina. Founded in 1916, it is built from stone and timber harvested from its land, and the school's logo, a seven-stoned arch featuring a keystone in the center, is patterned after one of the campus's prominent architectural features.

That logo provided the inspiration for the college's first-ever orientation program, aptly named Keystones. Like the school's logo, the new half-day program is built around seven modules: history and traditions, values, educational experience, academics, student life, courtesy, and efficiency. During the training, new employees are organized into teams of six and given a six-piece jigsaw puzzle that forms the image of a graduating student, a symbol of the ultimate goal of the school. Each keeps a piece of the puzzle and every six months they come back together for another two-hour training session that highlights another aspect of the seven modules.

Instead of sending a trainer to Montreat's satellite schools, those staff members come to the main campus for classes. "We had a lot of people who just didn't understand our heritage," Dean of Admissions and Financial Aid Lisa Lankford explained. "They didn't understand that their jobs were an important part of the entire educational show at Montreat. Now, they are starting to see."

So, when new employees at Dierbergs Family Markets hit the aisles or new cast members at Walt Disney World step onto their stage or new professors at Montreat College stand in front of their first class, they all have a sense of the community they have joined. The next goal of orientation is to link that picture to behaviors.

THE BEHAVIORS OF QUALITY SERVICE

In the past two decades, as Walt Disney World has defined and refined its four service standards, the Traditions program has also devoted more and more time to teaching cast members how to achieve them. The class introduces all of the standards, but is particularly focused on the elements of those standards that can be applied universally throughout the organization. That means training in the resort's core safety procedures and the basic elements of courtesy.

These universal procedures and behaviors are taught using a simple role-playing exercise for judging the guest experience called *Good Show/Bad Show*. A Good Show is anything leading to a positive guest experience and a Bad Show is . . . well, you've surely guessed the definition of that. These phrases, *good show* and *bad show*, have spread throughout the resort. So, when a cast member performs well, she is likely to get a thumbs-up from her supervisor and a hearty "Good show!" Conversely, when someone misses a service opportunity, he is likely to get an explanation of how to improve the "bad show."

Since the first priority of Quality Service is safety, new cast members are first taught exactly how to respond if an accident should occur. Then they learn accident prevention procedures ranging from evacuation routes to the use of fire extinguishers to emergency first aid techniques. Even the safe use of gestures is discussed; it would certainly be a bad show if a member of the landscaping staff whacked a guest while using his rake to point out directions.

Gesturing with a rake is rude as well as risky. So Disney University has spent a good deal of time defining courtesy in action and exploring how courtesy contributes to a positive guest experience. The result of these efforts is embodied in a list of actions called *performance tips,* which every Walt Disney World employee learns during the Traditions program.

Performance tips are a set of generic behaviors that ensure that cast members know how to act courteously and respect the individuality of each guest. The training addresses topics such as how to make a good first impression and offer a warm welcome. It explores the effects of posture, gestures, and facial expressions on the guest experience. And, it explains how tone of voice and the use of humor can contribute, or detract, from service delivery.

While the phrase "performance tips" may sound relatively innocuous, these tips pack a punch. At Walt Disney World, they have been translated into a set of behavioral

Walt Disney World Guidelines for Guest Service

Make Eye Contact and Smile!

- Start and end every Guest contact and communication with direct eye contact and a sincere smile.

Greet and Welcome Each and Every Guest

- Extend the appropriate greeting to every Guest with whom you come into contact.
    "Good morning/afternoon/evening!"
    "Welcome!"/"Have a good day."
    "May I help you?"
- Make Guests feel welcome by providing a special differentiated greeting in each area.

Seek Out Guest Contact

- It is the responsibility of every Cast Member to seek out Guests who need help or assistance.
    Listen to Guests' needs
    Answer questions
    Offer assistance (For example: Taking family photographs)

Provide Immediate Service Recovery

- It is the responsibility of all Cast Members to attempt, to the best of their abilities, to immediately resolve a Guest service failure before it becomes a Guest service problem.
- Always find the answer for the Guest and/or find another Cast Member who can help the Guest.

Display Appropriate Body Language at All Times

- It is the responsibility of every Cast Member to display approachable body language when on stage.
    Attentive appearance
    Good posture
    Appropriate facial expression

Preserve the "Magical" Guest Experience

- Always focus on the positive, rather than the rules and regulations.
- Talking about personal or job-related problems in front of our Guests is unacceptable.

Thank Each and Every Guest

- Extend every Guest a sincere thank-you at the conclusion of every transaction.
- Extend every Guest a thank-you or similar expression of appreciation as he/she leaves your area.

actions called Guidelines for Guest Service. The guidelines are summarized in seven sentences and serve a variety of purposes. First, they define behavior in terms of the guests. They create a common baseline for interaction with guests and demonstrate the elements of performance that perpetuate courtesy, Disney-style. Second, the guidelines communicate employee responsibilities. They make the company's expectations for service delivery clear to new cast members and they provide a basis for accountability. Fulfilling the performance guidelines is a condition of employment at Walt Disney World. Cast members who do not use them are subject to progressive disciplinary actions.

Walt Disney World's guest service guidelines serve one more important purpose. They showcase ways to customize service to individual guests. Practices such as smiling, greeting, and thanking guests are all well and good, but if these actions are restricted to rote, mechanistic behaviors, their effectiveness is severely limited. They are more properly seen as baseline-to-minimum expectations and a guide to the creation of customized service for individual guests.

The stories of how Walt Disney World cast members tailor service based on unique circumstances of the resort's guests are legion. There is the couple with the sick child who return to their room and find a personal get-well card from Mickey. It is the guest service guidelines that provide the jumping-off point for that level of service by cast members who use them to craft unique service moments for individual guests—not a bad return on seven short sentences.

After attending Disney Institute programs, Louisiana-based LifeCare Hospitals, a chain of eleven acute-care facilities operating in four states, created its set of organizational service standards labeled SKIP (Safety, Kindness, Image, Productivity). The company's 30-member implementation team linked those standards to employee behavior by designing its own set of performance tips.

For instance, for Safety, specific behaviors are recommended and taught, such as assuming ownership of potential safety hazards, walking visitors to their destinations, and offering assistance to people who look confused. For Kindness, performance tips include eye contact and smiling, maintaining a positive attitude and tone of voice, and specific phone etiquette. As at Walt Disney World, the three or four performance tips offered for each standard are not meant to be a comprehensive list of behaviors. Rather, LifeCare meant them as a baseline for employees to start translating the SKIP standards into everyday actions.

LifeCare's performance tips were rolled out with the SKIP standards in February 2000, with CEO Merlin Aalborg acting as the master of ceremonies. At the same time, the standards and performance tips associated with them became an integral part of the employee performance appraisal process. A Spotlight on Service recognition program was established in which managers who caught employees exhibiting the new service behaviors were able to give them SKIP award cards redeemable for LifeCare merchandise. In the SKIP Goals annual program, employees are asked to adopt one behavior for each standard and commit to displaying it on a consistent basis. And, finally, behavior in contradiction to the standards also became a cause for disciplinary action.

Sometimes the structure of a company can present a challenge to communicating the behaviors that will support its service theme and standards. For example, fast-growing Start Holding, a temporary employment agency based in Gouda, Holland, has more than 5,100 employees in 650 storefront offices located mostly in Holland, Spain, and Germany. To underscore the permanence of the service quality initiative, the company's executives positioned the effort as a leadership initiative that would ultimately be cascaded to all international as well as domestic operations. To launch its leadership initiative, the company brought its leadership team, board of directors, and four groups of district managers to the Disney Institute and then took more than 500 branch managers to an Institute program held at Disneyland Paris.

Start adopted a service vision, *We create careers*, and four service standards: Accessibility, Reliability, Service Provision, and Efficiency. But the company still needed to develop and communicate the performance behaviors that would help its widespread team of branch employees to deliver its brand of Quality Service. Start's answer was to create a system called the Service Box.

The Service Box includes a series of training and motivational videotapes, issued to leaders every two months, that explain and explore another aspect of Start's four Service Standards. Each office schedules a training meeting for its staff coinciding with the tape's arrival. Interestingly, the videos are relatively short, less than 15 minutes each, and are only designed to serve as a launching point for further learning. The remainder of each training session is devoted to brainstorming ideas for putting its contents to work on a day-to-day basis.

All of the ideas in each staff and operational area are collected and communicated via what Start calls Service Platforms—communications tools designed to leverage the creative effort of employees by sharing each office's solutions throughout the company.

THINK GLOBALLY, PERFORM LOCALLY

Anyone who has vacationed at Walt Disney World knows that the resort is a lot like a huge multiplex theater screening a variety of living, interactive movies at the same time. The movies are all entertaining. They are also all related by common production values, but each one tells a different story and uses a different theme. Within Walt Disney World, the Contemporary Resort has a radically different story and theme than the BoardWalk Resort. Epcot's Future World tells stories different from the 1940s Hollywood as recreated at Disney-MGM Studios. And so on.

The first tier of cast-delivered service, which includes the Traditions program and Service Guidelines, unites all cast members with common goals, language, and behavior, and offers a broad outline of what is meant by Quality Service. This tier helps create the multiplex theater that is Walt Disney World. But, to manage all the different films playing in the theater, the service mission and values must be driven down to the local level. That is done in the second tier of cast-delivered service at Walt Disney World with the creation and communication of *performance cultures.*

A performance culture is a set of *location-specific* behaviors, mannerisms, terms, and values that direct and enhance a cast member's role in any particular show. Performance cultures are developed and nurtured by the management and cast of the major resorts and parks of the Walt Disney World complex. Each performance culture includes its own mission, vision, and perform-ance values (which are, of course, aligned with the larger service theme and standards of the entire resort).

It might seem like a waste of time to create localized cultures instead of simply establishing a single organiza-tion-wide system, but there are some very good reasons for the practice. As we've already mentioned, the larger and more diverse the organization, the more difficult it is to create a single coherent culture that will make sense for everyone. A strong local culture speaks more directly to the day-to-day responsibilities of employees and strengthens the sense of ownership and involvement in the business unit. Like the performance tips, a local per-formance culture can be very detailed about the behav-iors that the local cast will share. And, perhaps most importantly for the delivery of Quality Service, it estab-lishes and reinforces the local show by tapping directly into the story and theme of the area. The result is a more memorable experience for guests.

One of the notable performance cultures at Walt Disney World can be found at Disney's Polynesian Resort. The Polynesian was part of Walt Disney's original vision for his new park in Florida and, open since 1971, it was one of the property's first two hotels. Renovated in the late 1990s, it is an 853-room resort set on a prime location near the Magic Kingdom. The South Seas theme and the style of the Polynesian are particularly relaxed and it is a favorite among guests for weddings and honeymoons.

A guest staying at the resort would surely be surprised to learn that the Polynesian has not always enjoyed the stellar reputation it has today. In fact, in the not-too-distant past, an assignment to perform there was usually not greeted with much enthusiasm. The property was not scoring high marks in terms of guest satisfaction. What turned the Polynesian around? The cast and its successful effort to create and maintain its own unique performance culture.

Under the leadership of general manager Clyde Min, the cast of the Polynesian undertook the challenge by taking cues from the style and theme of the hotel itself to build a new performance culture. They studied the island cultures of the South Pacific and created new connections between traditional island values and the performance culture of the hotel. The result was a new level of service based on *ho'okipa*, a word that describes Polynesian-style hospitality and the willingness to welcome and entertain guests with unconditional warmth and generosity.

The cast of the hotel created its own mission statement ("Our family provides a unique hospitality experience by sharing the magic of Polynesia and spirit of *aloha* with our guests and lifelong friends") and its own vision of the future. That vision called for a resort that would be a "lush

Disney's Polynesian Resort Values

Aloha
We love our fellow Cast Members and our Guests unconditionally.
SAMPLE BEHAVIORS: I will take an interest in my trainees and fellow Cast as individuals beyond work. I will greet and welcome every Guest and Cast member I meet with warmth and sincerity.

Balance
We strive for stability and vitality in our personal and professional lives.
SAMPLE BEHAVIORS: I will organize my day to accomplish everything and stick to my plan. I will assist others who need help if I finish early.

Courage
We pursue our beliefs with strength and perseverance.
SAMPLE BEHAVIORS: I will follow through with every dissatisfied Guest or problem until completion. I will give honest and caring feedback and coaching to others and accept it myself.

Diversity
We seek, value, and respect differences among our fellow Cast Members.
SAMPLE BEHAVIORS: I will respect and learn about the diversity of my fellow Cast and Guests. I will translate important information for Cast Members who only speak my native language.

Honesty
We deal with each other in a sincere and straightforward manner.
SAMPLE BEHAVIORS: I will turn in all items found and encourage others to do the same. I will be true to myself and admit when I am wrong or need help.

Integrity
We act in a manner consistent with our words and beliefs.
SAMPLE BEHAVIORS: I will be a positive role model at all times and adhere to departmental guidelines. I will replace negativity and criticism with a positive attitude.

Kina'ole
We provide flawless Guest service of our Polynesian Product.
SAMPLE BEHAVIORS: I will keep informed and updated on new information and procedures. I will do my job to the best of my ability the first time and every time consistently.

Mea ho' okipa
We welcome and entertain our Guests with warmth and generosity.
SAMPLE BEHAVIORS: I will smile and start conversations with Guests and Cast and use their names. I will introduce my trainees to my fellow Cast Members and show them around the property. I will go out of my way to make each Guest feel special with personal touches and interactions. I will assist and accommodate any Guest need or request to make them feel at home.

'Ohana
We treat each other as a family member, supporting, encouraging, and helping.
SAMPLE BEHAVIORS: I will encourage and motivate others to make our Cast and Guests feel special. I will be an available resource to support my trainees and fellow Cast Members.

Openness
We share information freely.
SAMPLE BEHAVIORS: I will make every effort to communicate to others who speak a different language. I will give recognition to my trainees and fellow Cast when a job is done well.

Respect
We treat others with care and consideration.
SAMPLE BEHAVIORS: I will respect the opinions, ideas, and feelings of others. I will pull my own weight to avoid impacting others in a negative manner. I will allow others to grow and learn from their mistakes.

tropical paradise known for creating magical lifetime memories." It also specified that the Polynesian would set a benchmark in its industry and be a place where guests and cast members would be willing to sign up on waiting lists for an opportunity to visit and work.

To support the resort's new mission and vision, the cast adopted a series of values that furthered the themed nature of the resort by mixing traditional corporate values, such as diversity and openness, with true Polynesian values, such as *'ohana*, or family, and *aloha*, or love and warmth. These values were then linked directly to cast behaviors.

The cast also identified and attacked barriers to guest satisfaction. Concerned that the check-in required a long wait and that guests were not arriving to an experience that welcomed them properly to the warm and rich culture of the Polynesian Islands, the cast redesigned the process. Front Desk, Bell Services, and Valet cast members partnered to create a new check-in sequence that incorporated a cast-led tour of the lobby providing plenty of information about the amenities of the resort and an opportunity to ask questions. No additional costs were incurred and the time each guest stood at the front desk was significantly reduced along with the corresponding wait for service.

The effort to revitalize the Polynesian Resort quickly bore fruit. Guest satisfaction measures improved across the board, registering increases from 21 percent to 68 percent. The number of repeat guests rose far enough to put the property in the running for a first place finish in Walt Disney World's Guest Return rankings. Cast satisfaction ratings rose from percentiles in the 70s into the mid- and high 90s, and the resort's costs in terms of workman's compensation and safety accidents dropped until they were the lowest at Walt Disney World. Here's one more statistic that speaks volumes for how cast attitudes toward the resort changed: On Bring Your Child To Work Day in 1996, eight children visited the property; two years later, 113 children came to see where their parents worked.

The use of local performance cultures to interpret and add value to organizational service themes and standards is starting to take hold at Lehigh Valley Hospital and Health Network (Their PRIDE service standards are discussed in chapter 2.) Impressed by the performance culture he saw at Disney's All-Star Resorts during a Disney Institute program, internal Organizational Development consultant Jack Dunleavy brought the concept back home to use at the departmental level. As we write this, Mr. Dunleavy has helped establish five performance cultures at LVHHN and one in the private practice of one of the hospital's physicians.

In Radiology, for instance, the staff adopted a local subtheme linked to their work: "We *create lasting images* of caring, compassion, and service excellence by providing answers with our diagnostic tests for customers of all ages." The group even created its own song, sung to the tune of the theme song from the television show *Cheers*. The departmental staff interpreted LVHHN's service standards in light of its own work and learned and adopted performance tips to support their delivery.

A similar effort occurred among LVHHN's valet assistants, who are responsible for operating the free valet parking service at the hospital. Their subtheme:

"*We create awesome arrivals and fond farewells* by providing memorable first and last impressions with all customer groups." Again, the team broke service standards down into behaviors. This time, they redesigned the guest experience around the three segments of the valet parking process: the arrival of the guest, the identification of their needs and assisting them properly, and their departure.

BUILDING YOUR PERFORMANCE CULTURE

Building cultures is not a science. In fact, it is a fairly mysterious process that when done well is capable of uniting the energy and emotions of the entire workforce in a single, focused direction. Anyone who has ever been exposed to such a culture can tell you that they can accomplish magical levels of service. Just as often, maybe even more often, culture-building efforts fail, leaving behind high-minded statements that do not reflect any existing reality. While we can't give you a guaranteed formula for creating a performance culture, we can give you some insight into the development process as it has evolved at Walt Disney World.

If you take a closer look at the work that produced new performance cultures at the Polynesian Resort and Lehigh Valley Hospital and Health Network, you will see that the implementation efforts were accomplished in three phases. First, new visions and missions were designed to align the workforce to the business unit in a more powerful way. Second, the values connected to the mission and vision

Six Tips for Culture Building

1. **Keep it simple.** Everyone must feel comfortable with the culture. Leave room for individuality and personality.
2. **Make it global.** Everyone at the site, including management, must buy in.
3. **Make it measurable.** Create specific guidelines and make them a part of the performance assessment process.
4. **Provide training and coaching.** Incorporate the elements of the culture into employee training and ongoing performance coaching. Encourage peer-to-peer coaching.
5. **Solicit feedback and ideas from the team.** Foster a sense of ownership and expand the pool of creative input by allowing employees to contribute to the show.
6. **Recognize and reward performance.** Build employee motivation through formal and informal reward and recognition programs.

were identified, articulated, and linked to behavior on the job. And finally, the workforce was turned loose to create the Quality Service vision it had designed.

To create a new vision and mission capable of uniting everyone working within an organization or business unit, it only makes sense that everyone, or at least a team that represents everyone, be enlisted in the effort. They need to define their work in relation to customers and the service theme and decide what role they will play in the accomplishment of that theme. As an example, think about the ways in which the Polynesian's mission is similar to and at the same time unique from Walt Disney World's service theme. The team also needs to consider how employees relate to each other and how they relate to customers. At the Polynesian, the cast decided to be a family and customers became guests and lifelong friends. Finally, they need to cut the tethers and dream about how their unit would look if it could become anything they wanted. This blue-sky thinking becomes the basis for a shared vision for the future.

The creation of a set of shared performance values is intimately connected to the establishment of vision and mission. Some management thinkers believe values precede mission and vision, others suggest the opposite. In either case, creating shared performance values is an important foundational element from which employee behavior and actions will follow. Identifying values should also be a team effort. The team needs to consider what values are already at work in the organization, what new values are required to support the culture, and how well they will meet the service needs of customers. As the cast of the Polynesian did, they also must consider how to link values to action by establishing behaviors that reflect the values and how those behaviors will be measured.

The final phase of building a performance culture is to give employees the freedom to begin living it. They need to consider how they will achieve their mission and vision, how their jobs affect service delivery, and how they can improve that delivery. Witness the reinvention of the check-in process at the Polynesian. Employees also

Quality Service Cues

Make a memorable first impression: First impressions are lasting ones. Start sending the right messages to prospective and new employees from the very first point of contact.

Communicate the heart and soul of the organization first: Your heritage, values, service theme, and service standards are more important than the paperwork associated with new hires. Use new employee orientation sessions to communicate your organizational vision and culture.

Speak a service language; wear a service wardrobe: How you look and how you speak communicates an image in the customer's mind. Make sure that your appearance and language reflect your brand of Quality Service.

Establish a set of performance tips: Performance tips are generic behaviors that ensure that employees know how to act courteously and respect the individuality of each guest. They form the baseline for delivering and measuring Quality Service performance.

Build a performance culture: Performance cultures are sets of location-specific behaviors, mannerisms, terms, and values that direct and enhance an employee's role in a specific business unit. They use shared values, visions, and missions to help the workforce optimize and customize service delivery.

need to begin the never-ending work of translating mission and strategy into action, and the practicing of behaviors that reflect the performance values. Only then will the work of building a performance culture begin to produce results.

End Notes

[1] See Robert Lacey's *Ford: The Men and the Machine* (Little, Brown, 1986) for a history of the Ford family and company. Henry Ford's quote appears on p. 305.

[2] The quote appears in Richard Schickel's *The Disney Version* (Ivan R. Dee, 1997), p. 178.

[3] See Bob Thomas' *Walt Disney* (Hyperion, 1994) for more detail on the development of the Disney Art School. The quote appears on p. 124.

[4] *Ibid.*, p. 143.

[5] *Walt Disney Famous Quotes* (Disney Kingdom Editions, 1994), p. 80.

[6] This portion of Michael Eisner's speech appears in a video segment of Walt Disney World's Traditions training class.

[7] Training, October 1999, p. 58.

[8] For a more detailed description and photographs of the Casting Center, see Beth Dunlop's *Building a Dream: The Art of Disney Architecture* (Abrams, 1996). The quotes from Robert Stern, Beth Dunlop, and Tim Johnson appear on pp. 77–80.

[9] Danie Boshoff's quote appears in *Fourways Crossing: Substance of Excellence* (Pick 'n Pay, 1998).

[10] Richard Parks' quote appears in Leon Rubis' article "Disney Show & Tell" in the April 1998 issue of *HR Magazine*.

CHAPTER 4

THE MAGIC OF SETTING

Walt Disney was an Oscar magnet. He was personally nominated for Academy Awards on 64 occasions, the most nominations ever recorded. He won 32 Academy Awards, also the most ever. After a couple of dozen trips into the spotlight, picking up Oscars probably began to feel a little routine to Walt, but the first, which he accepted in 1932, must surely have been a thrill. That year, Walt received the first award ever presented in the new category of Best Cartoon for "Flowers and Trees," the twenty-ninth film in the *Silly Symphonies* series and the first ever made using a new color process called Technicolor.

The innovative use of color in a cartoon was the main reason that "Flowers and Trees" was such a sensation among both audiences and critics, but it is notable for another reason. The short film showcased the possibilities of setting like no other cartoon ever had before. In it, two young trees fall in love, but their happiness is threatened by a jealous rival, in this case, a gnarled stump. The old stump sets the forest afire to separate the lovers, but is itself consumed. The forest returns to life and the young lovers are wed. The woodland setting of trees and flowers and the music, by Mendelssohn and Schubert, communicate the story to the audience. In fact, the setting, in this case, the forest, which would have provided only the background in another cartoon, had suddenly become the entire film.

In 1938, Walt and the Disney studios picked up two more Academy Awards. This time, one of the studio's inventions, the multiplane camera, received an award in the Scientific and Technical category and the first film made with the camera, another *Silly Symphony* entitled "The Old Mill," won for best cartoon. The multiplane camera represented another major step in capturing the full potential of setting. The camera allowed Disney animators to overcome what Walt's biographer Bob Thomas called "the essential flatness of the animated film."[1] The camera could be pointed and moved through stacks of cels and glass plates, creating the same effect as a live-action camera moving through a set. The result was a depth of setting that had never been seen before; it created a fantasy world that was more convincing because audiences saw it the same way they saw life. "When we do fantasy, we must not lose sight of reality," explained Walt.[2]

In 1940, *Fantasia* was released and Walt's innovative use of setting was again much in evidence. Broomsticks marched and flowers and mushrooms danced. *Fantasia* also broke new ground in the use of sound, an important element of setting. The film used Fantasound, which recorded music using several microphones and played it back through a corresponding number of speakers. Walt received an Academy Award for the technical breakthrough, but the outbreak of World War II closed down *Fantasia*'s foreign markets, and the expensive audio equipment needed to properly present the film made domestic theater owners reluctant to show it. *Fantasia* cost $2.2 million to make, more than four times the cost of the average live-action film at that time, and it flopped on first release. Two decades later, in the 1960s, it was re-released, took audiences by storm, and was proclaimed a classic of animation.[3]

Walt's insistence that animated films must be believable to the audience to be effective was translated directly into the settings of Disneyland. You might think that Walt's idea for the first theme park was met with instant acclaim, but that was not the case. In the late 1940s, as Walt became more and more intrigued with creating his own kind of amusement park, he got less and less support for the idea. Walt's brother Roy, his longtime business partner and the holder of the company's purse strings, did not see the financial merit in this risky, long leap beyond their current business and was reluctant to fund the idea. In 1952, Walt got tired of waiting and, with his typical drive, went ahead without the rest of the company. He created a new corporation, WED Enterprises, Inc., and funded it by borrowing against his insurance policies and by selling his vacation home in Palm Springs. He also hijacked the first class of Imagineers right out of the Disney animation studios, stashing them in empty offices and workshops around the property to work on the park.

Since the people who designed and built Disneyland came from the animation side of the business, they treated its settings as integral and important parts of the park from the very start. Disneyland was going to be a living movie that its guests would experience by moving through it. And, as in animated films, to make that vision come to life, the audience had to have the opportunity to become totally immersed in the experience. Every detail of the setting had to support the story.

"Walt was asked why he worked so hard to make it all look realistic," remembers Imagineer Tony Baxter. "He said what we're selling is a belief in fantasy and story-telling, and if the background wasn't believable, people wouldn't buy it."[4] With the benefit of 20/20 hindsight, the soundness of Walt's thinking is obvious. The audience didn't simply buy the idea of Disneyland; they fell in love with it.

The role of setting in the Disney theme parks was revitalized in the mid-1980s when Michael Eisner assumed leadership of The Walt Disney Company. Eisner didn't know much about theme park construction, but he knew how to create compelling entertainment.

"He was a movie guy—ABC, Paramount," explains Peter Rummell, who headed up Disney's construction projects worldwide. "For months, every time he saw PUD [planned unit development] on a plan, I'm convinced he thought it meant 'producers using drugs.' But what he did bring was a total understanding of what Disney is; what its strength is; what it represents to the world. You all know the horribly overused real estate maxim 'location, location, location' as a key to success. Eisner's chant very quickly became 'entertainment, entertainment, entertainment.' He was consistent and unrelenting."[5]

Two weeks into his new job, Eisner suggested building a hotel shaped like Mickey Mouse. It wasn't feasible, but to Disney insiders, the freshly hired CEO's willingness to swing for the fences signaled a whole new ball game in terms of setting. Shortly thereafter, Eisner scrapped plans for two new, but architecturally mundane, hotels at Walt Disney World. It was a gutsy move that risked a long-term relationship with a valued development partner, but it paid off. The 1,514-room Walt Disney World Dolphin Hotel and the 758-room Walt Disney World Swan Hotel replaced the canceled hotels. Designed by world-renowned architect Michael Graves, they created a new standard for setting at Walt Disney World.

The Swan and Dolphin signaled a renaissance in Disney architecture. Soon, the best architects in the world were working on commissions for the company. At Walt Disney World, resorts such as the Grand Floridian, Wilderness Lodge, BoardWalk, and Yacht Club and Beach Club (the latter designed by Robert A. M. Stern) took setting to a whole new level. "Our hotels became experiences and entertainments in themselves," wrote Eisner in his book *Work In Progress*. "Successful as our hotels are in artistic terms, the simplest tribute to them comes from our guests. To this day, the occupancy rate at each of them runs in excess of ninety percent—the highest in the world."[6]

SETTING DELIVERS SERVICE

If you ask the typical businessperson how their company delivers service to customers, they will surely mention people and processes (the topics of the last and next chapters respectively) as primary delivery systems. But, the idea that an organization's setting can somehow deliver service is more obscure. Can a setting really deliver anything at all and if so, how does it deliver service?

In fact, setting can deliver both the physical and psychological aspects of service. At Walt Disney World, for example, there are many attractions where cast members will load and unload guests, but the bulk of the service experience is delivered during the ride by the setting itself. In these days of e-commerce, we are witnessing a transformational shift in physical service delivery from employees to setting. After all, when you connect to the Internet and buy books, CDs, or any one of what seems like a zillion other products and services available online, you are served by a setting, that is, the Web site from which you are buying. In most e-commerce transactions, the customer is the only human involved in the sale. The setting and electronic processes are delivering service. Employees are involved in the creation of the site and, after the fact, in the fulfillment of orders.

The use of setting to deliver the psychological aspects of service is similarly common. All organizations, knowingly or unknowingly, build messages to their customers into the settings in which they operate. Picture a luxury car dealership and a used car lot. Now, a theme park and a carnival. And now, a designer clothing retailer and an outlet store. In each pair, people are buying similar products—cars, entertainment, and apparel. But, in each case, the setting in which they buy these products is communicating a great deal about the quality of the products and services customers can expect, not to mention the price they are willing to pay.

The simple fact is that everything, animate and inanimate, speaks to customers. Not only does everything speak, it also acts upon customers. The messages delivered by setting change customers' perceptions about the products and services that we sell. As R. Buckminster Fuller, one of the most original thinkers and inventors of the twentieth century and the creator of the geodesic dome on which the 180-foot tall Spaceship Earth at Epcot is based, aptly said, "You can't change people. But if you change the environment that the people are in, they will change." [7]

The point of all of this is that setting is a critical element of the Quality Service Cycle and it is vital that settings be designed and managed to effectively communicate and deliver service to customers. A brief definition: *Setting is the environment in which service is delivered to customers, all of the objects within that environment, and the procedures used to enhance and maintain the service environment and objects.* More simply, setting is the stage on which business is conducted.

At Walt Disney World, the primary setting is the entertainment resort "inside the berm." The phrase originated at Disneyland, where Walt had a simple landscaped hill, a berm, constructed around the property to physically delineate the boundaries of the property and to block external distractions, such as highways and buildings, which might interrupt the living movie he was building. "I don't want the public to see the world they live in while they're in the park," said Walt. "I want them to feel they're in another world." [8] The sharp contrast

The Components of Setting

Architectural design
Landscaping
Lighting
Color
Signage
Directional design on carpet
Texture of floor surface
Focal points and directional
 signs
Internal/external detail
Music/ambient noise
Smell
Touch/tactile experiences
Taste

between the world on the outside of the hill bordering Disneyland and the one inside the hill prompted cast members to start identifying being at work as being inside the berm. It only takes a short tour of Walt Disney World to see how seriously every detail is managed inside the berm.

As you have probably noted, setting is not restricted to physical properties. The Disney Web sites that describe and promote Walt Disney World are part of the setting and so are the telephone systems that take reservations and communicate with guests, and the Disney gift kiosk in the Orlando airport. Setting also extends to other area businesses. Elaborately themed monorails and motor coaches communicate service messages to guests, too.

As the definition states, setting also includes the objects within the environment. At Walt Disney World, that means the furniture in the hotel rooms, the utensils in the restaurants, the trees and flowers on the property, and of course, the attractions in the parks. All these objects contribute to the delivery of entertainment to guests. If the bed is uncomfortable, the silverware clunky, the plants sparse, and the rides jerky, who would want to return for a second visit? How many instances of poorly designed setting would it take to drive a guest away forever? These are questions to which few organizations want to find answers.

Finally, setting includes the work of maintaining and enhancing the environment and the objects within it. Even the best-designed setting must be continuously maintained and improved. Rides must be kept in good repair, rooms must be cleaned, plants fed and watered, etc. A poorly maintained setting is just as telling as a poorly designed one.

If it all sounds like a lot of work, it is. Creating practical magic is hard work and it is a tenuous business that is entirely dependent on attention to detail. Listen to how Imagineer John Hench describes it:

> Interestingly enough for all of its success, the Disney theme show is quite a fragile thing. It just takes one contradiction, one out-of-place stimulus to negate a particular moment's experience . . . tack up a felt-tip brown-paper-bag sign that says "Keep Out" . . . take a host's costume away and put him in blue jeans and a tank top . . . replace that Gay Nineties melody with rock numbers . . . place a touch of artificial turf here . . . add a surly employee there . . . it really doesn't take much to upset it all.
>
> What's our success formula? It's attention to infinite detail, the little things, the little, minor, picky points that

others just don't want to take the time, money, or effort to do. As far as our Disney organization is concerned, it's the only way we've ever done it . . . it's been our success formula. We'll probably be explaining this to outsiders at the end of our next two decades in the business.[9]

One organization that does not need further explanation about setting is Metairie, Louisiana–based East Jefferson General Hospital. East Jefferson, a 525-bed, not-for-profit hospital, began its own Quality Service journey at the Disney Institute and used the experience to implement a wide variety of improvements in its setting.

Committed to a service theme of "Providing care and comfort is our highest mission," the hospital undertook a series of design changes in everything from the landscaping of its grounds to a new design for its Intensive Care Unit (ICU). Staff began parking in a neighboring parking lot and taking a shuttle to work, so that patients and visitors could use the parking lot on the hospital's grounds. When a new parking garage was erected, it was designed so guests would not have to walk more than 35 steps before encountering a staff member.

East Jefferson's ICU is a model of service delivered through setting. For this 20-bed critical care area, East Jefferson created two rows of 10 rooms lining a wide corridor. Almost the entire front wall of each room is glass, curtained for privacy, that can be swung open like a door allowing X-ray and other bulky equipment to be moved near the patient. There is an X-ray development station in the unit, so films can be processed and read on the spot.

The ICU's interior room walls are lined with shuttered bins and cabinets. Everything a critical care nurse needs to care for the patient is within a step or two. So that nurses can stay in constant contact with patients, the traditional nurse's station has been redesigned into a series of counters featuring telephones and computers that are located just on the other side of the glass walls of the patients' rooms. Patients and on-duty nurses are almost always within eyesight of each other. In 1992, the patient care and efficiency of operation built into East Jefferson's ICU setting won the annual ICU Design Award jointly given by the Association of Healthcare Architects, the Foundation of Critical Care Medicine, and the American Association of Critical Care Nurses.

IMAGINATION + ENGINEERING = IMAGINEERING

It is impossible to discuss setting without taking a few minutes to talk about Walt Disney Imagineering. The word *Imagineering* was coined by Walt himself. When asked about Disney's success, he replied, "There's really no secret about our approach. We keep moving forward—opening new doors and doing new things—because we are curious. And curiosity keeps leading us down new paths. We're always exploring and experimenting . . . we call it Imagineering—the blending of creative imagination and technical know-how."[10]

Imagineering is also one of The Walt Disney Company's business units. With more than 1,600 employees, the Glendale, California–based division is responsible for the creation of all Disney resorts, theme parks and attractions, real estate developments, location-based entertainment venues, and cyberspace/new media projects. When you marvel at Walt Disney World's rides, with their detailing and special effects, you are paying tribute to the Imagineers' work. They are the people who first imagine and then design and build settings. Their motto: *If you can dream it, you can do it.*

How do Imagineers create settings that deliver Walt Disney World's service theme and standards? Vice-chairman Marty Sklar gave a concise answer to that complex question when he created a list of setting design principles he labeled Mickey's Ten Commandments. "They came out of the Imagineering process and what I've learned from my principal mentors, Walt Disney and John Hench," Marty explains. They set the stage for the rest of this chapter.

1. *Know your audience:* Before creating a setting, obtain a firm understanding of who will be using it.
2. *Wear your guest's shoes:* That is, never forget the human factor. Evaluate your setting from the customer's perspective by experiencing it as a customer.
3. *Organize the flow of people and ideas:* Think of setting as a story and tell that story in a sequenced, organized way. Build the same order and logic into the design of customer movement.
4. *Create a "wienie":* Borrowed from the slang of the silent-film business, a wienie was what Walt Disney called a visual magnet. It means a visual

landmark is used to orient and attract customers.

5. *Communicate with visual literacy:* Language is not always composed of words. Use the common languages of color, shape, and form to communicate through setting.

6. *Avoid overload—create turn-ons:* Do not bombard customers with data. Let them choose the information they want when they want it.

7. *Tell one story at a time:* Mixing multiple stories in a single setting is confusing. Create one setting for each big idea.

8. *Avoid contradictions; maintain identity:* Every detail and every setting should support and further your organizational identity and mission.

9. *For every ounce of treatment provide a ton of treat:* Give your customers the highest value by building an interactive setting that gives them the opportunity to exercise all of their senses.

10. *Keep it up:* Never get complacent and always maintain your setting.

With the Imagineer's Commandments in mind, let's take a look at two major uses of setting: its ability to send messages to customers and its use as a guide to the service experience.

SENDING A MESSAGE WITH SETTING

As guests move from one attraction to another at Walt Disney World, they are told new stories. These stories, or themes, change from attraction to attraction and from park to park. They extend into hotels and restaurants. Setting plays a primary role in the delivery of each of those. When setting supports and furthers the story being told, it is sending the right message.

One of many examples of this can be seen at the entrance to the Magic Kingdom. When you arrive at the main gate to the Magic Kingdom, you proffer your pass and enter the park through turnstiles. You are now in an outdoor lobby, which features phones and restrooms, and once past the lobby, you walk into one of two short tunnels leading into Main Street's Town Square. The tunnels are lined with posters "advertising" the attractions within. As you leave the tunnels, even first thing in the morning, you smell freshly made popcorn, which is made in carts placed near the tunnel openings. The experience of entering the park is designed to remind guests of the experience of entering a movie theater. There is the ticketing and the turnstile, the lobby, the halls to the screening rooms lined with posters displaying the coming attractions, and even the popcorn.

As stories change, so must their setting. Walt Disney World is noted for the beauty of its landscaping, but no one who enters the Haunted Mansion would call it well manicured. As guests line up to enter the ride, they find themselves under a canopy that cuts off the bright Florida sunlight before it reaches earth. They pass an abandoned cemetery in which the leaves lie where they had fallen from the trees and the plants are wild and stunted from the lack of light. Inside the mansion, dust and cobwebs are everywhere. This level of dishevelment is tough to maintain. The park purchases dust in five-pound bags and sprays it over the attraction with a kind of reverse vacuum cleaner. The cobwebs are made from a liquid that is strung up by a secret process.[11]

The resorts on the property also make good use of setting messages. The Wilderness Lodge is located right next to the Contemporary Resort, but the modern world never imposes on the Lodge's American West setting. Guests can't see the Contemporary; the views are purposely blocked. They enter the lodge along a winding road that is flanked by tall pine trees and dotted with old-fashioned streetlights and a BEAR CROSSING sign. Walk straight through the main lobby and out of the building and the long view over a completely undeveloped lake reminds guests of the open spaces and natural wonders of the U.S. National parks. Lest you get the impression Disney can control everything, notice the Spanish moss hanging from the pines on the property. It doesn't grow out West, but no matter how hard the landscaping team tried, they couldn't get it to stop growing in Florida. They bowed before Mother Nature.

Disney isn't the only organization that tells stories. Every organization tells its own unique stories to its customers and those stories must be supported and furthered by setting. For example, New York–based professional services powerhouse PricewaterhouseCoopers (PwC) sends a compelling message to prospective employees by borrowing Walt Disney World's setting. The largest accounting, auditing, and consulting firm in the world, PwC employs 155,000 people globally and uses an internship program to attract more than 1,000 of the best and the brightest college students to its doors. A significant portion of PwC's interns end up working full time for the firm, so getting students to accept invitations to the program is an important prerequisite to getting the best new hires available. That's why PwC brought the setting of Walt Disney World, along with Disney Institute training, into the picture.

In 1998, PwC concluded its annual internship program by bringing its entire class of interns to Walt Disney World for five days of training and fun that they call *Discover the Magic*. An instant hit with students, the program sends a compelling message about how much PwC values their potential. "The trip seemed to cap off what would be an exciting internship from start to finish," said Kevin Post, an intern from Lehigh University. "The idea of traveling to Florida at the end demonstrated an enormous commitment. It was apparent that PwC recognized that their greatest asset was the individual."[12] The program has been continued ever since.

Further proving the point, since starting *Discover the Magic*, intern acceptance rates continue to rise. And, in 1999, a Universum International survey found that the consulting firm was rated the first-choice employer out of 180 companies by 3,100 business students in 46 universities.

Another organization that counts students among its customers is Dover, Delaware's Wesley College, an 1,800-student private school affiliated with the United Methodist Church. After attending a Council of Independent Colleges seminar at the Disney Institute,

Wesley administrators decided to take better advantage of their setting during the open houses held to introduce prospective students and their families to Delaware's oldest private college (founded in 1873). "We needed to help the admissions staff do more than point to a building and say 'That's the science building,'" explains Acting Vice President for Academic Affairs Lorena Stone. "We needed to tell a memorable story during our campus tours."

The new open house tour is not much longer than the old one, but it includes a new path and scripts designed, as Dr. Stone says, "to bring the college to life for students." For instance, the tour now starts in the amphitheater, where the college's graduation ceremonies take place and prospective students get a picture of where they could be four years later. At the Cannon Building, where the science classes are held, the admissions guides tell the story of Annie J. Cannon, a noted woman astronomer who taught at the school and invented an identification system for stars still in use today. And, at the Campus Community School, which offers educational programs for local children, the teachers-to-be in the audience get a good look at the field experience they can gain without leaving the campus. At Wesley, the setting is helping to sell the college to prospective students.

A good exercise to better understand the messages sent by setting is to visualize a store that you patronize or better yet, actually visit it. Drive up to the front entrance and look at the signage and landscaping. What impression do they convey about the business within? Enter the business. Look at the entryway. Is it clear how to proceed?

Is it clean and orderly? What does it tell you about this organization? Continue to observe the setting throughout the process of making a purchase. At each step, think about what the setting is telling you. Now, return to your own organization. Approach it like one of your customers and repeat the exercise. What does your setting tell customers?

Sometimes, looking through a customer's eyes takes an adjustment in perspective. Disney Imagineers have been known to don kneepads and crawl around the parks to experience them from a child's perspective. The next time you walk down Main Street in the Magic Kingdom notice how low to the ground the windows of the shops extend. They allow children to see the displays as comfortably as adults can.

As John Hench declared, telling a story through setting means getting the details right. An organization can't send customers a believable message regarding Quality Service unless every detail of setting supports it. An overflowing trash basket or a dead plant can undercut a message about the quality of your product or the care for your customers in a single glance. A sign with missing letters or misspelled words tells customers something about you. A Web site with links that lead nowhere or a Web page that won't load properly communicates a negative message. When you are telling a story to your customers, make sure that your setting is sending messages that reinforce your story.

GUIDING THE GUEST EXPERIENCE

Setting can do much more than simply create an impression in a customer's mind. It can also be used to assist customers through the service experience. Cues in the setting explain where customers have been and where they are going. They signal changes and give instruction. When the components of setting are used to instruct customers, we say they are guiding the guest experience.

Anyone who has been to the Magic Kingdom already knows that the theme park is laid out around a central hub. The hub is a common element in Disney's parks. The design came to Florida directly from Disneyland, where Walt Disney first used it to guide guests.

"This is the hub of Disneyland, where you can enter the four realms," explained Walt to his future biographer Bob Thomas during a preopening tour of the park in 1955. "Parents can sit in the shade here if they want, while their kids go off to one of the other places. I planned it so each place was right off the hub. You know, when you go to a world's fair, you walk and walk until your feet are sore. I know mine always are. I don't want sore feet here. They make people tired and irritable. I want 'em to leave here happy. They'll be able to cover the whole place and not travel more 'n a couple of miles."[13]

Walt's hub design does more than ease tired feet. It also directs guests. At the Magic Kingdom at Walt Disney World, there is one entrance to the park, which leads guests onto Main Street. From Main Street there is only one direction to go, forward toward the hub that offers direct access to each of the park's lands and serves as central return point for movement throughout the park. Behind and looming over the hub is a beacon, that is, Cinderella Castle, the most visible feature inside the park. The castle draws guests up Main Street and into the heart of the park. It is the wienie, the most important of all the visual magnets in the Magic Kingdom.

Guests can also move between lands in the Magic Kingdom and when they make the transition, they experience another concept borrowed from the world of film: the cross-dissolve. A cross-dissolve is used to get the movie audience from one scene to the next. The Disney Imagineers explain how it works in the parks:

> A stroll from Main Street to Adventureland is a relatively short distance, but one experiences an enormous change in theme and story. For the transition to be a smooth one, there is a gradual blending of themed foliage, color, sound, music, and architecture. Even the soles of your feet feel a change in the paving that explicitly tells you something new is on the horizon. Smell may also factor into a dimensional cross-dissolve. In a warm summer breeze, you may catch a whiff of sweet tropical flora and exotic spices as you enter Adventureland. Once all these changes are experienced the cross-dissolve transition is complete.[14]

The spaces between any two distinct areas and other peripheral areas, such as parking lots and waiting rooms, are especially important places in which to use setting for service delivery. Customers usually have low expectations of these in-between areas, and small investments in effort can yield exceptional impressions.

The central hub and cross-dissolve are two major examples of how setting guides guests at Walt Disney World, but there are many more setting cues that direct guests. Landscaping is an important signaler of direction and signage is an obvious guide. Color also gives directional cues. For instance, ice cream wagons in the park are often blue, signaling a cool refreshment. Popcorn wagons are red, signaling a warm treat.

The University of Chicago Hospitals & Health System (UCH) is a top-rated, 639-bed medical complex located on Chicago's South side. In 2000, *U.S. News & World Report* ranked it among the top 15 hospitals in the nation and number one in its home state. As a Disney Institute client, UCH considered every detail of the service experience and expanded its definition of setting well beyond its property boundaries to ensure that its setting was doing as good a job guiding its patients as its expert staff was.

"We flowcharted the home-to-home experience—even with details like what signs were on the expressway and what kind of support materials were provided in advance," Vice President and Director of UCH's Center for Advanced Medicines Jeff Finesilver explains, "We also created a valet parking experience—the Center for Advanced Medicine now operates the busiest valet parking experience in the entire City of Chicago. We also paid attention to architectural features, from sky-bridge signage to elevator and hall signage—all the onstage and backstage areas—to maintain decor and facilitate a smooth experience for visitors."

The use of setting as a tool for guidance is not confined to physical space. It works in virtual space as well. We have all had the experience of being shuffled through a voicemail labyrinth only to reach a dead end that leaves no alternative but to hang up and start over again. When customers call your organization, how well does the phone system guide them to their desired destination? Web sites can be even more annoying. Every online shopper has had the experience of filling an electronic shopping cart full of goods only to have it dumped off a cyber-cliff on the way to the checkout. Is your site designed to be intuitive for customers? Does it cut customers off in the middle of their transactions? Setting needs to be managed wherever your customers meet you.

APPEALING TO ALL FIVE SENSES

Taking full advantage of setting in order to enhance the customer experience means designing for all five senses. People understand their environment and gather impressions through sight, sound, smell, touch, and taste. Each sense offers an opportunity to support and enhance the show created for the guests.

Sight

About 70 percent of the body's sense receptors are located in our eyes, making sight the greatest transmitter of setting. Obviously, as we've already noted in our examples, Walt Disney World is designed to display delightful and entertaining views wherever guests look. Sight lines are a major consideration. What you see and, just as important, what you don't see, from your hotel window or from anywhere else on the property is carefully planned.

Color is considered throughout the parks. Many guests notice the unusual purple-and-red color scheme on the directional signs on the public roads in and around Walt Disney World. As an experiment, flags of different colors were once set out on the property and guests were asked which ones they remembered seeing. Purple and red were the colors they recalled most often.

The Imagineers are experts in the use of color and have created their own "color vocabulary," which defines how certain colors and patterns act on guests. "Different projects call for different uses of color," explains Nina Rae Vaughn, Imagineering illustrator. "If a project wants to communicate 'fun,' as in [Disneyland's] Mickey's Toontown, I will experiment with bright colors, applying the brightest of brights against the darkest of darks. If the idea says 'adventure,' like the Indiana Jones Adventure, I will use colors that shout action and excitement. These are hot reds and oranges, with shades of complementary colors like blues, that make the hot colors even more vibrant."[15]

Sound

Sounds are caused by vibrations of infinitely varying pitch, quality, and loudness. In designing setting, the only vibrations guests hear should be good ones. If you have ever found yourself unable to banish from your mind the tune from a Disney attraction, such as "It's a Small World After All," you know the power of sound in setting. As John Hench says, "People don't walk out of attractions whistling the architecture."[16]

To get an idea of how sophisticated the sound systems get at Walt Disney World, listen to the parades on Main Street. A single cast member working a mixing board controls the audio portion of the parades. Speakers on the floats are synchronized with 175 speakers along the parade route, so that no matter where you choose to view the parade, you are surrounded by an appropriate audio track. How does the soundtrack move in tandem with the parade? There are 33 sound zones along the parade route and sensors embedded in Main Street. As each float triggers a sensor, the soundtrack for that float "moves" along with it.

Perhaps the most entertaining use of sound on the property is the *Sounds Dangerous* attraction at Disney–MGM Studios starring actor-comedian Drew Carey. This 3-D audio adventure follows Drew as he attempts to solve a mystery. More than half the popular show occurs in total darkness and all of the action is communicated through sound alone.

Smell

There are about 5 million receptor cells in the human nose and it is only a short trip from there to the brain. Smells are stored in our long-term memory. In fact, scientists have found that if you associate a list of words with smells, you will better remember the words. At Walt Disney World, smells are used to help deliver magical memories.

We've already mentioned the popcorn carts positioned at the entrance tunnels to the Magic Kingdom. Vendors don't sell much popcorn at 8:30 in the morning, but the corn is already popping. The smell of popcorn communicates the living movie message of the park. The bakery on Main Street purposely pumps the scent of fresh baked goods into the street to support the story of America's small towns.

Touch

The skin is the largest organ in the human body and touch is the sense that resides there. Whether it comes through the hands or feet or face, people get lots of data from the tactile properties of the environment and the objects within it. At Walt Disney World, the sense of touch is considered in the walkways, attractions, hotels and restaurants, and throughout the rest of the property.

The touch of water is an integral part of many attractions. Water splashes on guests to heighten the experience at Catastrophe Canyon during the Disney-MGM Studios Backlot Tour and in Jim Henson's MuppetVision 3-D show. The water parks and resort pools are all about touch. Young guests love the surprise fountains all around the property. They spend hours trying to anticipate from where and when the next stream of water will shoot. Touch, or the lack of it, is also the sense that we play to when the elevator in The Twilight Zone Tower of Terror drops out from under and plunges thirteen stories. To intensify the experience, the Imagineers created a ride that drops even faster than the speed of free fall.

Taste

There are about 10,000 taste buds in the human mouth and each taste bud contains roughly 50 taste cells that communicate data to our brains. Walt Disney World's eateries cater to as many of those cells as possible with a wide range of dining experiences.

In addition to more than 300 restaurants featuring a vast selection of food, menus change as the setting dictates. From turkey legs in Frontierland to the saltwater taffy at Disney's Boardwalk, tastes follow setting. World Showcase at Epcot is a 1.3-mile tour of global cuisine, where it is just a few short steps from the sushi in Japan to freshly made fettuccine in Italy.

Sight, sound, smell, taste, and touch—designing and delivering Quality Service means appealing to all of your customer's five senses.

ONSTAGE AND BACKSTAGE

Another major consideration in the delivery of quality customer experiences through setting is the separation of onstage and backstage activities. In chapter 1, when we introduced the concept of practical magic, we talked about the distinction between being onstage and backstage at Walt Disney World. "Onstage" is all public areas of the park where guests roam freely and service is delivered. "Backstage" is all of the behind-the-scenes areas where guests don't go, a place where all the mechanisms and technologies that run the property (and all the people that run them) reside and where cast members can move freely and prepare themselves to go on stage. Both are part of the overall setting.

The first and best reason to keep onstage and backstage areas separated is that anything that does not support and enhance the Quality Service experience will, by definition, detract from it. No hotel guest needs to see the laundry or the power plant. Most restaurant-goers would find stacks of dirty dishes an unappetizing sight.

Second, it is an unnecessary expense to design and maintain backstage areas to the same standards as onstage areas. In fact, expensive lighting fixtures and moldings don't stand much of a chance of surviving in corridors where mechanized carts and forklifts are moving supplies.

Finally, the presence of customers is a distraction to employees at work behind the scenes. An electrician repairing a faulty circuit breaker doesn't have attention to spare for a guest. Equally important, employees need somewhere that they can be backstage to relax. Giving cast members a real break is important. You won't see or hear Disney movies and music playing in the employee cafeterias and break areas on the property. The cast members come to those places to eat and relax; they are not working.

At the Magic Kingdom, the separation of onstage and backstage required some careful planning. Built on wetlands, where the water table is on or very close to the surface of the ground, the park did not have the luxury of basements and subbasements. Instead, the land had to be raised so that the ground floor of the site could be used for utility purposes. The public area of the park was built on top of it, on the second floor. The ground floor back-stage area is called the Utilidor (Disney-speak for "utility corridor").

Utilidors are work spaces and so are clean, practical, and composed of materials and painted in colors that you won't see onstage, such as cinder blocks and painted institutional grays and greens. Unlike the pathways above, they run in straight lines designed to get cast members to their destinations as quickly as possible. Using the Utilidor under the Magic Kingdom, for example, cast members can don their costumes and get anywhere in the park in just a few minutes. That way there is no need to ever worry about a pirate popping up in Tomorrowland.

The Utilidors are connected to other backstage areas "above" the ground. These areas are often located only a few feet from the onstage areas, but thanks to the use of visual screens, guests never see them. On Main Street, for example, the side streets often end in a suitably decorated gate or doorway with a polite sign that signifies a cast-only area. On the other side of that door is an environment that looks more like the back of a supermarket or a manufacturing plant than a theme park. The view from inside the park is blocked by the design of the set itself. If a building needs a second story to screen the view, it is built.

The Wolfsburg, Germany–based Volkswagen Group, which borrowed its setting from Walt Disney World to create a memorable dealer launch for the New Beetle, has built the onstage/backstage distinction into its Volkswagen Marketplace, the ideal design for its dealerships worldwide. One feature of the Marketplace plan is the construction of backstage areas for the sales staff. This is a place where they can get offstage, take a break, or have meals. It doubles as a meeting and training area.

"Salespeople need a place where they can let their hair down without appearing rude to the customers, so we moved these functions behind the scenes," Volkswagen of North America's Bill Gelgota says. "We want to control our environment like Disney does. The worldwide design standard helps us control and reinforce the experience we think the customer wants to have."

With all of Disney's emphasis on the separation of the onstage and backstage areas of setting, it was slightly ironic to discover that guests wanted to visit backstage. It turns out that they were intensely curious about how Walt Disney World's stories come to life. In response to repeated requests for a look behind the curtain, Disney created a dozen behind-the-scenes tours that are, of course, as carefully scripted as the onstage entertainments. If your customers are curious to see how your products and services are created, a well-crafted, behind-the-scenes look may be just the ticket to improve their service experience.

The Volkswagen Group also accommodated its customers' desire for a behind-the-scenes look at their dealerships. The company understood that purchasing a new car takes only a few hours and car owners are likely to spend much more time than that in the service department while they own their vehicle. As a result, customers want to be assured that the service component of their purchase, delivered in the back end of the dealership, would be as pleasant as the sales component delivered in the front end.

The carmaker built that assurance into the setting of its ideal dealership. One of the important design elements of VW Marketplace is the opening of the sales floor onto the service area. In this way, new buyers are able to see the service areas of the dealership, get a feel for where they will spend time during service visits, and see the product—the new cars—being prepped for delivery. The sales process, by the way, has been redesigned to take advantage of this seamless connection between sales and service. When customers buy cars, they are given a tour of the service area and introduced to the dealer's service advisors.

MAINTAINING THE SETTING

We've spent most of this chapter describing elements and principles of setting that are usually addressed during design and construction phases. But, there is one more important subject to discuss before moving on: the maintenance of setting. Once you have created the perfect setting, the work of keeping it that way begins and continues as long as the setting is in use. Maintenance means more than just keeping the setting clean. It also means protecting it from damage, and repairing wear and tear.

After onstage and backstage field experiences, Institute facilitators ask program guests to estimate the size of the Walt Disney World maintenance cast. The replies vary widely, but the correct answer is always a surprise. There are more than 55,000 people maintaining the setting at Walt Disney World. That is because maintenance is an integral part of every cast member's role. From Michael Eisner on through the ranks, you will never see a cast member pass by a piece of trash on the property or ignore a physical detail of the parks needing repair.

It is part of the culture to keep Walt Disney World clean, and the habit can be traced directly back to Walt himself. "When I started on Disneyland," he once recalled, "my wife used to say, 'But why do you want to build an amusement park? They're so dirty.' I told her that was just the point—mine wouldn't be."[17]

There is also, of course, a large dedicated maintenance staff at Walt Disney World. They work around the clock to keep the parks' settings pristine. Streets are cleaned daily; the restrooms every 30 minutes. There are horses on Main Street, but you have to be on the spot to see any of their natural byproducts. The costumed custodial cast is never far behind. Maintenance technicians are on hand to make sure that all of the attractions run smoothly during the day. The staff swells into the hundreds after the parks close and the scheduled maintenance and repairs are made.

Maintenance is a significant expense in any large organization and so should be designed into the setting whenever possible. When journalist Scott Kirsner visited backstage at the Magic Kingdom, he was struck by the technology employed to maintain the landscape.

> Based on input from the weather stations, MaxiCom's PC-based software determines how much water each of the property's 600 zones needs. Each has up to 10 individually watered beds; when a message comes in from the gardeners that a row of azaleas at Disney–MGM Studios is drying out, the horticulturist will increase the amount of water delivered there each

night. When a torrential rainstorm passes over the property, the MaxiCom system adjusts by watering less—about 50 automated rain cans that measure by hundredths of an inch are scattered around the property and plugged into the network. "Every morning at 1:25, we download the data to cluster control units (CCUs) situated around the property," says [horticulture manager Scott] Shultz. The CCUs manage the sprinkler timers, which govern 50,000 sprinkler heads between them. Shultz's crew also prowls the property daily in a van equipped with a laptop and cellular modem, troubleshooting the whole system—one of the most sophisticated large-scale irrigation setups anywhere.[18]

In the watering of the landscape, and throughout the property, the cast and maintenance technology combine to create a continuous and consistent focus on keeping the setting in perfect repair. As a result, the setting supports and enhances the guest experience and delivers quality service.

Quality Service Cues

Define your setting. Setting is the environment in which service is delivered to customers, all of the objects within that environment, and the procedures used to enhance and maintain the service environment and objects.

Tell your story through the setting. Walk through the service experience in your organization wearing the customer's shoes. Observe and critique the setting and align its messages with the service story you want to tell.

Guide the customer experience with setting. Consider the directional aspects of setting. Make sure the physical layout of your organization (or Web site or phone system), interior design, and signage keep customers on the track to Quality Service.

Communicate Quality Service to all five senses. Customers build their impressions of you using all of their senses. Send your service message with appeals to a customer's sight, sound, smell, touch, and taste whenever possible.

Separate onstage and backstage. Screen business functions that do not involve customers so that they do not interrupt the delivery of service. Give employees a backstage space to rest and relax.

Maintain your setting with a consistent, comprehensive effort. Use the design process to build maintenance into the setting and enlist every employee in the maintenance effort.

End Notes

[1] The phrase appears on p. 134 of Bob Thomas' *Walt Disney: An American Original* (Hyperion, 1994).

[2] The quote appears on p. 200 of Richard Schickel's *The Disney Version* (Ivan R. Dee, 1997.)

[3] For more on *Fantasia* and all of the Disney animated films, see Bob Thomas' *Disney's Art Of Animation: From Mickey Mouse To Hercules* (Hyperion, 1997).

[4] Tony Baxter quote appears on p. 14 of Beth Dunlop's *Building a Dream* (Abrams, 1996).

[5] *Ibid.*, p. 16.

[6] The quote appears on p. 221 of Michael Eisner's *Work In Progress: Risking Failure, Surviving Success* (Hyperion, 1999).

[7] The quote appears in "The Disney Approach to Quality Service for Healthcare Professionals, Participant's Manual."

[8] Walt Disney's quote appears on p. 90 of *Walt Disney Imagineering* (Hyperion, 1996).

[9] John Hench's quote appeared without attribution in "The First Twenty Years: From Disneyland to Walt Disney World, A Pocket History," which was distributed to cast members in 1976.

[10] Walt Disney's quote appears on p. 9 of *Walt Disney Imagineering* (Hyperion, 1996).

[11] See Birnbaum's *Walt Disney World 2000: the Official Guide* (Hyperion, 1999) for descriptions of the Disney attractions. The haunted mansion is featured on p. 102.

[12] Kevin Post is quoted in "The Price of Admission," *Human Resource Executive,* June 16, 2000.

[13] The quote appears on p. 13 of Bob Thomas' *Walt Disney: An American Original* (Hyperion, 1994).

[14] The quote appears on p. 90 of *Walt Disney Imagineering* (Hyperion, 1996).

[15] *Ibid.*, p. 95.

[16] *Ibid.*, p. 130.

[17] See *Walt Disney: Famous Quotes* (Disney's Kingdom Editions, 1994), p. 29.

[18] See Scott Kirsner's "Hack the Magic" in the March 1998 issue of *Wired* magazine for a good look at the technological systems used to run Walt Disney World and for the quote.

CHAPTER 5

THE MAGIC OF PROCESS

A kid in a garage. It is the starting place of many a contemporary business legend. Apple Computer, Amazon.com, and Cisco Systems were all started in their founders' home garages. Walt Disney was once a kid in a garage, too.

In 1920, at the age of 18, Walt got his first taste of animation at the Kansas City Film Ad Company. He was drawing figures, which were used in advertising films seen in local movie theaters. In what would become a personal trademark, Walt felt constrained by the primitive technology used on the job and he pushed himself and the company's head, A. Vern Cauger, to improve the quality of the company's minute-long ads. He even convinced Mr. Cauger to lend him a stop-action camera, which he brought home to a "studio" that he and his brother Roy had hastily constructed in the family garage.

The result of the loan was 300 feet of cartooning that satirized the poor road conditions in Kansas City. Walt sold it for thirty cents a foot to the Newman Theater Company. The audience liked Walt's cartoon so much that he was engaged to produce one each week. The Newman Laugh-O-gram was born, and soon after, Walt founded a new company to make them, Laugh-O-grams Film, Inc. This company would not survive very long, but Walt had become an animator.[1]

Alone at night, working in the garage, Walt surely did not think much about process. In those first animations, the images were drawn, cut out, and pinned to a background in poses meant to simulate motion, and photographed. The resulting film was crude, with flat, one-dimensional characters, and of course, sound and color were still years away. Walt simply decided on a subject and strung enough drawings together to create the number of feet of film needed. But, if you had asked the young animator to articulate his methods, he would have described processes—the mental process of telling the film's story and the physical process of making the film itself. Walt was using process to deliver entertainment.

By the 1930s, the role of process in the creation of Disney animation was much more explicit. In the fast expansion following the success of Mickey Mouse, Walt could no longer remember every detail of each cartoon in production or take a hand in every decision. He needed to formalize an approach to the daily operations of the company, so he began to construct the processes that would manufacture and deliver the Disney brand of entertainment.

Previously, Walt and artist Ub Iwerks would huddle in an office and create the continuity script and drawings for a cartoon. They would emerge with a complete work and hand it over to the staff to be animated and produced. Now the cartoons were produced using a team-based creative process in which no one person dominated. A flexible Production Unit was assembled in which a director would oversee the overall project, a stylist would create the mood and atmosphere, a storyman would tell the tale, and a story sketchman would draw the first rough visuals. The characters would go into development—their voices and bodies created and refined. Now a sort of crude movie was made, a story reel combining the story sketches and sound tracks. Throughout the work, the team, Walt, and others outside the team, would examine and think and argue and contribute ideas. And that was just the beginning—huge chunks of work, such as the layout, animation, sound track, and filming, were still to come.

The Disney process did not tame animation. Like any creative endeavor, it remained chaotic and, according to insiders, ever-changing. "In spite of constant efforts and persistent claims, Walt never did build an organization in the strictest sense of that word. What he built was a loosely unified group of talented people with particular abilities who could work together in continually changing patterns. They did this with a minimum of command and a maximum of dedication. What Walt wanted was the greatest creative effort—not the most efficient operation," wrote Frank Thomas and Ollie Johnston, two of the Nine Old Men, as the Disney animating supervisors during that golden era of animation were known.[2] The funny thing is that that description sounds exactly like the structures that so many companies are trying to create today. Walt had built a flexible organization around a process-based structure.

To simultaneously organize work and, instead of stifling energy and creativity, to actually enhance it, is an accomplishment rarely achieved. To accomplish it in a niche business like animation was even more unusual. That's one reason why biographer Richard Schickel wrote: "That any young man was willing to attempt such a business must remain as a permanent tribute to his stubbornness. That Walt Disney, alone of all the men who went into animation, was able to emerge from it a full-fledged tycoon (several made a bit of money out of it eventually) must stand as a tribute to organizational abilities of a very high order."[3]

When it was time to design Disneyland, Walt brought the same process orientation he had applied in the studio out into the physical world. There was one important difference now. To make an animated film, you ran it through the process once and created a finished product that could be viewed over and over without additional work. In a theme park, each process had to run continuously and turn out the same product each time. (It is, in fact, an odd kind of process industry. Instead of refining petroleum or mixing chemicals, it makes entertainment.) Walt knew that the key to delivering quality service in a living movie meant designing a defect-free process and flawlessly repeating it.

There was one big advantage to working with repetitive processes that were delivering a standardized product and Walt realized it immediately. He told a reporter:

> The park means a lot to me. It's something that will never be finished, something I can keep developing, keep "plussing" and adding to. It's alive. It will be a live, breathing thing that will need changes. When you wrap up a picture and turn it over to Technicolor, you're through. Snow White is a dead issue with me. I just finished a live-action picture, wrapped it up a few weeks

ago. It's gone. I can't touch it. There are things in it I don't like, but I can't do anything about it. I want something live, something that would grow. The park is that. Not only can I add things, but even the trees will keep growing. The thing will get more beautiful year after year. And it will get better as I find out what the public likes. I can't do that with a picture; it's finished and unchangeable before I find out whether the public likes it or not.[4]

Walt could fine-tune Disneyland's processes to his heart's content, and he did. He called this effort at continuous improvement "plussing" and he applied it everywhere in the park. He would wear old clothes and a farmer's straw hat and tour the park incognito. Dick Nunis, who was at the time a supervisor in Frontierland, remembers being tracked down by Walt during one of these visits. Walt had ridden the Jungle Boat attraction and had timed the cruise. The boat's operator had rushed the ride, which had ended in four and a half minutes instead of the full seven minutes it should have taken.

"How would you like to go to a movie and have the theater remove a reel in the middle of the picture?" demanded Walt. "Do you realize how much those hippos cost? I want people to see them, not be rushed through a ride by some guy who's bored with his work."

Dick and Walt took the ride together and discussed the proper timing. The boat pilots used stopwatches to learn the perfect speed. Weeks went by until one day Walt returned. He rode the Jungle Boats four times with different pilots. In the end, he said nothing, just gave Dick a "Good show!" thumbs-up and continued on his way.[5]

Plussing is still an important part of the Disney culture. If something can be made better, it's done. Disneyland Paris was originally named Euro Disney, but to Europeans, the target audience, the word *Euro* signified currency and commerce. It did not create the picture intended in the guests' minds and so, it was "plussed."

When the Disney Store chain was first getting off the ground in the late 1980s, Michael Eisner starting visiting newly opened locations on weekends à la Walt. He studied the details, weeding out substandard products and analyzing the lighting, presentation, and service experience from the guest's perspective. Frank G. Wells, Disney's late president and COO, insisted that the stores adopt service standards and offer Traditions-like employee training. The two executives knew that building a successful chain required a standardized process that could be transplanted to every new store and that lived up to the Disney name. And, said Eisner, "If the boss cares, I had long since learned, then everyone else cares." The process-building and plussing efforts paid off. By 1991, there were 125 stores generating more than $300 million in revenues.[6]

PROCESS AND COMBUSTION

Processes, in their broadest meaning, are a series of actions, changes, or functions that are strung together to produce a result. They combine human (cast) and physical (setting) resources in various ways to produce different outcomes. A car is produced using a process that combines parts and labor in specific sequences on an assembly line. An appendectomy is performed using a process that combines medical staff and an operating room in a sequence of actions. All organizations can be thought of as a collection of processes.

A process delivers a result. That is, it delivers some outcome, such as a product or service. In fact, more than three-quarters of service delivery in most industries and institutions is process-based. And, since Quality Service is all about delivery, it is critical to pay special attention to processes.

In the Quality Service Cycle, *processes* are the policies, tasks, and procedures that are used to deliver service. We are now talking about the steam engine of the Quality Service Cycle train. If that engine does not run, it does not matter how friendly the engineer acts or how attractive the railroad cars look, the train will still not move and the passengers will not pay their fares. Processes power the Quality Service train.

We can take the railroad analogy one step further and talk about the workings of the engine on the train. Engines are driven by combustion. A diesel or gasoline engine is powered by internal combustion. The fuel is fired inside the engine; it explodes and moves the pistons. In a steam engine, the combustion takes place outside the engine in a boiler that creates pressurized steam that in turn moves the pistons. Service processes are more like a steam engine. The combustion is externally produced . . . by guests. For the purposes of Quality Service, guest-produced combustion is the best kind. When guests are powering the engine, we know that the process is focused properly on their needs.

When service processes work smoothly, their key combustion points are controlled. Guests are satisfied and the Quality Service engine runs without a hiccup. However, when a service process misfires, the combustion point is out of control. Guests are inconvenienced and unless their problems are solved, combustion points can easily turn into explosion points. Identifying and controlling combustion points are an important part of delivering service through process.

The best way to identify key combustion points is to study your guests. What do they complain about? Where do they get stuck during the service experience? What are the common problems they face when moving within your organization? The answers to these questions are *combustion statements*. Combustion statements are important clues to the process issues you need to address to deliver magical service.

Let's examine some common combustion statements:

- **"This is taking too long!"** Anyone who has ever stood in line at the post office or grocery store knows this lament. What does it indicate? It tells us that we have a problem with the flow of the service experience that needs to be solved.
- **"No one knows the answer!"** We've all been faced with guests who have been bounced from place to place in search of an answer to a question. When you hear this, it means that the communication process . between cast and guest has broken down.
- **"My situation is different!"** Creating a standardized process is a great way to serve the typical guest, but what about the guest who doesn't fit the standard pro-

file? When you hear this it means the process itself is not able to accommodate certain guests.

- **"I'm stuck in a dilemma!"** Finally, processes are not infallible and sometimes they just don't work as planned. When you hear this it means that the service process needs repair.

These combustion statements are not uncommon at Walt Disney World. You have probably heard them from your customers, too. That's because these four examples relate to service process issues that are universal. Customer flow, employee-to-customer communication, customers with special needs, and poor process design are typical combustion points in service processes, and in the remainder of this chapter, we will take a closer look at how to keep them from becoming explosion points.

GUEST FLOW

"These lines are too long!" Walt Disney World's guests hate long lines. They are the single most frequently criticized problem in the theme parks. On Disneyland's opening day, a day that Walt Disney afterward labeled "Black Sunday," guest flow was a fiasco. Counterfeit tickets turned what had been planned as an invitation-only event into a mob scene as an estimated 33,000 guests overwhelmed the park. Every street within ten miles of the front gate was jammed with traffic. One of the first questions Walt addressed after Black Sunday was how to better manage those lines.[7]

"Long lines" is a service process issue that relates to the flow of the guest experience. If you run a Web site, the flow of service can be impeded by slow-loading pages or the capacity of the site to handle a rush of customer activity. If you operate a manufacturing company, the flow might be blocked by a certain assembly task or a part shortage or an inefficient machine. No matter what the specific service or product being delivered, "wait time" is the enemy we are all fighting.

Solutions to the wait-time conundrum tend to fall into three separate categories. To minimize wait time, we can optimize the operation of the product or service, optimize the flow of guests themselves, or optimize the experience of being in the line itself. At Walt Disney World, all three service process solutions have been implemented.

- *Optimizing the operation of product and services* means manipulating the use of your assets to minimize waits. Consider giving guests access to your facilities earlier or later than usual. You can also cut wait time by extending access on a selective basis, such as opening some services prior to others or opening key areas earlier than the rest of the organization. Another idea is to provide special access to your best guests. In this way, you can reward loyalty and reduce wait times simultaneously.

  One program designed to optimize the operations at Walt Disney World is called Surprise Mornings. On selected days, the Magic Kingdom, Epcot, and the Disney–MGM Studios open an hour early for those guests staying at the resorts on the property. This group of valuable customers gets a chance to experience the parks when they are relatively uncrowded and the program also helps reduce the number of guests enjoying the parks at peak hours. E-Ride Nights are another guest flow solution. This after-hours program charges a nominal fee for admission to the top nine attractions. Again, after-hours access to popular rides cuts peak demand, and the reduced ticket price helps control the cost of extended operation. The Rope Drop program is a third example of optimizing the operation. Here, selected services, dining areas, and retail stores open prior to the opening of the rest of the park. Guests get early access and can eat, shop, and otherwise prepare for the day and be ready for their favorite rides as soon as they open.

- *Optimizing guest flow* means enabling guests to self-manage their movement through the service experience. These techniques are designed to give guests the gift of time. They give your guests choices about how they will spend their time and provide those choices up front, before they get caught in a wait. They also include educating guests about the benefits of certain choices and monitoring flow continually so you can offer them accurate information.

At Walt Disney World, guests learn about their options before they arrive at the entrances to the parks themselves. The bestselling Birnbaum's official guides to the parks offer suggestions for getting the most value from Disney vacations. The brochures and guides provided at the parks also include plenty of tips for making the most of a visit. One feature you will find at a central location in the Walt Disney World parks is the Tip Board. An idea developed by the cast, the Tip Board lists the major attractions within the park and estimates the current wait at each. Updated regularly, Tip Boards allow guests to plan their travels in the parks and minimize the time they spend standing in lines. (Wait-times are slightly overestimated. A shorter-than-expected wait is much preferable to a longer-than-expected one.) Greeters also play an important role in helping guests manage their visits. These cast members are dedicated information sources whose role is to guide guests among the many entertainment choices in the parks.

- *Optimizing the queue experience,* finally, means managing the otherwise unavoidable wait time in a service process in order to maximize the guest experience and minimize discomfort. We can accomplish this feat by testing products and services to be sure wait times are minimized before opening them to the public. It is also important to clearly explain wait times at the start of a process and, as mentioned above, do your best to stay under the maximum time quoted. You can instruct and prepare guests to move through a process efficiently, and during waits, use the opportunity to educate, inform, and entertain them. You can also measure the lengths of the waits and make sure your cast members understand their impact on guests.

At Walt Disney World, Cast Preview Days introduce the staff to new attractions and help to ferret out process flaws before guests arrive. Sneak Peeks are pilot tests in

---

Factors Affecting Guest Perceptions of Wait Time

Disney Institute client University of Chicago Hospitals (UCH) surveyed patients about expectations regarding patient wait times. Although some wait time is a reality, most UCH patients in the study commented less on the length of the wait than how the wait was handled. Three important dimensions relating to patient care are:

- **Access**—Patients want access to care and are frustrated by voice mail, scheduling difficulties and restrictions.
- **Respect**—Patients describe a strong need to be recognized and treated with dignity.
- **Information communication**—Patients express fear that they are not being completely informed.

---

which a limited numbers of guests get an advance look at new attractions and which further refines the process before the grand opening. Like the parks' Tip Boards, each attraction has its own wait time posting that guests can see before they step into the line. And, finally, we make sure to build theme and entertainment into the queues themselves. The cast members are trained to entertain and otherwise occupy the attention of guests waiting in line and the setting is designed to make waits seem shorter. For instance, as guests wait to enter Jim Henson's MuppetVision 3-D show at the Disney–MGM Studios, they are entertained by a 12-minute preshow. Muppet characters move across a bank of television monitors and drop hints about the show to come.

This is all just a sampling of tactics employed to defeat the dreaded lines at Walt Disney World. The battle against wait time goes ever on, though the latest initiative,

Disney's FASTPASS Service, may have finally won the war. First introduced in 1999, FASTPASS is an innovative computerized reservation system. When guests arrive at a FASTPASS attraction, they can choose the traditional wait in line or swipe their admission pass in a turnstile which in turn produces a pass good for a one-hour usage period. They simply return during the specified hour and are processed through a short, dedicated line directly into the preshow or boarding area of the attraction.

FASTPASS eliminates the infamous lines altogether. Guests can visit less crowded areas, shop, or stop for a bite to eat while waiting for their ride, instead of standing in line. It is currently in use in 19 of the most popular attractions in the four Walt Disney World parks and it is a hit with guests. The process is being refined and will be rolled out in the parks on a broader basis.

St. Simon's Island, Georgia–based Rich-SeaPak Corporation is one Disney Institute client that is hard at work removing wait time from its order management process. A subsidiary of the largest family-owned frozen foods manufacturer in the United States, Rich Products Corporation, Rich-SeaPak is a leading producer of frozen seafood and snack products, with more than one thousand associates at plants in Georgia and Texas. The company enjoys a broad customer base that includes grocery stores, wholesale clubs, restaurant chains, and food-service clients processing 50,000 to 75,000 orders annually.

Over the years, however, SeaPak's order process had grown unwieldy. Customer orders moved between several information systems that were developed at different times. The legacy systems had been joined, but were unable to create a continuous, optimized flow. SeaPak associates had to move between systems to locate orders and there were "stop and gos" where orders paused in the process. The company knew that if it reengineered the process, it could improve its service delivery and increase profits.

A cross-functional team of 25 SeaPak associates, who visited the Disney Institute to study quality service and creativity, rethought how orders are managed from the customer's initial contact through fulfillment, billing, and the payment of invoices. They created a less complex, integrated information system capable of eliminating pauses by processing orders in a continuous flow, providing instant order information access to customers at any point in the process, and eliminating errors in the billing process. The new order process will cut days off SeaPak's order flow. It also solves a common problem among food products companies; it will track inventory and pricing variations in real time, eliminating billing errors, with the goal of producing perfect invoices every time.

Creating the perfect open-house process was the goal of a 15-member team at North Carolina's Lees-McRae College, a 600-student private institution known for its performing arts program. Located deep in the Appalachian Range in Banner Elk, in the northwestern corner of the state, 100-year-old Lees-McRae is the highest college east of the Mississippi River. After attending the Disney Institute, the college decided that the three major open-house programs it holds each year for prospective students and their families needed some sprucing up. "There was nothing actually wrong with the way we had been conducting open houses," Vice President for Enrollment and Student Development Alan Coheley explained. "They were nice and helpful, but they weren't providing a 'wow,' a memorable experience for our guests."

To build some wows into the program, the open-house team decided to expand their view of the process and considered the entire guest experience from the arrival of an invitation to visit the college until the completion of the program itself. They then used storyboards, a technique discussed in the next chapter, to rework the open houses in three phases.

First, the team refined the preparation phase of a guest visit by redesigning elements such as the directions to and descriptions of the area and the program that guests receive in the mail. Second, they improved the arrival phase and started welcoming guests before they set foot on campus through the use of techniques such as sending a representative from the college to meet and greet families as they checked into the local hotel. And, finally the team reengineered the entire on-campus portion of the experience by adding a county fair theme to their open houses. Now, as guests move from location to location around the campus, they find a new attraction in each spot. These attractions inform and entertain guests at the same time. Even the menus for the programs were adjusted to reflect the kinds of foods you might find at a fair. The new open-house process gives the college an extended control over guest experience, builds some fun into the college search process for prospective students, and not least of all, ensures that when it comes time to make their final choices, Lees-McRae will still stand out in their minds.

CAST-TO-GUEST COMMUNICATION

"When does the three o'clock parade start?" This is a common guest query. It is so frequently asked that Disney University uses it as an example in the Traditions program and the Disney Institute uses it as well. The guests who ask this question are not looking for the pat answer. What guests are really asking is what time the parade will get to a certain location or where the best place to see it is or what its route is. In fact, the only wrong answers to the question are "Three o'clock" or a wisecrack.

Answering guest questions is a regular task in all organizations. How well and how efficiently these questions are fielded plays a big role in how guests rate the service experience. Is there any person on the planet who likes being bounced from place to place in search of an answer to what should be a simple question? The only varying factor is exactly how long people will hang on before losing their cool altogether. When that happens, a combustion point has become an explosion point.

On a property the size of Walt Disney World with an annual guest list of millions of people, effective guest communication is a critical element in service delivery, and much of that communication flows directly from the cast to the guests. Disney's performance tips require cast members to seek out guest contact, to listen and answer questions and offer assistance. But, it is not enough to simply command the cast to help guests, they must have the information they need to fulfill that task. Accordingly, there a wide variety of service processes aimed at preparing the cast to give guests the answers they need on the spot. These processes are designed to provide the right information in the right manner at the right time.

Some of the techniques are meant to disseminate information throughout the property. These include information that every cast member needs to know about Walt Disney World. A weekly newspaper, *Eyes & Ears*, is one way information is communicated property-wide. It has a bigger circulation than many community newspapers; 60,000 copies are distributed each week. Pocket-sized fast-fact cards are printed and distributed so that cast members have information about new attractions and special events at their fingertips. In recent years, the corporate intranet has been used. Michael Eisner periodically e-mails cast members.

Creating awareness among 55,000 cast members about all of the property's attractions and resources is an important process. When Disney's All-Star Movies Resort, catering to value-oriented guests, was preparing to open to the public, the resort held an "Open Mouse" and invited all Walt Disney World cast members, their families, and friends. In addition to refreshments and character appearances, the resort staff made sure their fellow cast members learned about the new hotel by creating an on-site tour contest. Each guest received a map of the site that was stamped at locations along the tour route. They turned the maps in at the end as entries in prize drawings.

Job-shadowing techniques can teach cast members about other areas of the property. When the cartering and convention services team at Disney's Coronado Springs Resort wanted to spread the word, they planned Convention Mousenap, during which high-performing cast members from around Walt Disney World were "mousenapped" and spent a day learning about the resort's capabilities. Internal trade shows are also held periodically and give cast members a chance to share their best practices throughout the organization. And, there is a central repository for information at the Walt Disney World Library and Research Center, which includes more than 3,000 Disney-related volumes and an archival collection of news clippings, press releases, statistical information, and other publications for the exclusive use of the cast.

There also are techniques designed to communicate site-specific information to the cast members who perform in each area of our parks and resorts. These help avoid information overload by communicating detailed information to each specific site's cast members, but not to the larger population.

Some of the site-specific techniques are simply scaled-down versions of the property-wide techniques. The 1,000 bus-transportation cast members get a biweekly newspaper, *Bus Bulletin*. And, the cast of the retail stores get Merchantainment Cue Cards, a collector card series similar to the fast facts cards, which feature a Disney character on one side and character trivia along with policy and procedures on the other.

Other site-specific communication techniques are designed for separate performance cultures. For instance, cast members get up-to-the-minute information by attending preshift meetings that are known around the property as "homerooms." After finding that cast members who started work between shifts were sometimes missing important information, the cast of The Land Pavilion attraction in Epcot took the homeroom concept a step further. They started videotaping the daily meeting and created a backstage area where all employees could watch it before they started their daily performance.

Speaking of backstage areas, it is almost impossible to walk through any of them without seeing the ubiquitous bulletin board. Backstage Communication Boards convey loads of information on changes in policy and procedure, recent improvements, anticipated guest counts, and overall business performance. Similarly, for last-minute news flashes, Electronic Message Display Boards are positioned so cast members will see a message before walking onstage.

Few of Disney's processes for enhancing cast-to-guest communication are complex. That is not a coincidence. The important point is not how high-tech your communication methods are, but how well and how thoroughly they prepare your staff to assist customers. In fact, the less time and money spent on communication the better—it is, after all, an overhead cost. Concentrate instead on providing critical content and memorable presentations in the simplest ways possible.

Of course, sometimes the simplest communication method is also a high-tech solution. Witness Houston, Texas–based Crown Castle International Corporation (CCIC). Since its founding in 1994, CCIC has raced to a leading role in the wireless communications industry with an aggressive series of acquisitions. By June 2000, this Disney Institute client owned and leased more than 11,000 wireless tower sites reaching 68 of the 100 largest wireless markets in the United States, 95 percent of the population of the United Kingdom, and 92 percent of the population of Australia. The world's largest independent owner of shared wireless communication infrastructure, CCIC leases this infrastructure to cellular telephone service providers, television and radio broadcasters, and other customers needing wireless networks.

As CCIC grew, it expanded its vision far beyond leasing space on towers to world-class turnkey wireless services. CCIC customers can choose to contract for a complete network or any portion thereof. This breadth of service, the international nature of the business, and the rapid addition of acquired assets added up to a unique cast-to-guest communication conundrum. CCIC had to assist its technical personnel in the consistent and reliable delivery of the full range of complex service offerings no matter where they were located.

After discovering that each of its customers had a different definition of what turnkey service meant, CCIC began mapping every detail of every product and service process it delivers. In essence, it created process modules that its engineers could combine to build a customized solution for each customer.

"By taking all the processes necessary and breaking them down into definable areas and steps, we formalized our approach to service delivery across the company," explains COO John Kelly. The process modules guide employees through the design and implementation of the service package and ensure high quality and fast delivery. And, LiveLink, a feature on the CCIC corporate intranet, delivers all of that knowledge directly to its engineers. The information that CCIC's cast needs to serve their customers is delivered where and when they need it.

SERVICE ATTENTION

Have you ever gotten lost in a voice mail system that offers a long litany of options that don't fit your particular need and that has no instructions for connecting to a live person? How did you respond? Perhaps you picked a choice at random or blindly punched the phone's operator or star key hoping to transfer to a human being or maybe you just hung up. How did you feel about that service experience? When you get stuck in an unresponsive phone system, you are traversing a service process that simply does not work for you. It might work for a majority of the people who use it, but that isn't much consolation to those who can't use it.

In chapter 2 we introduced the idea that every guest should be treated as a VIP. That is, a very important *and* very individual person. Acknowledging and incorporating the individual needs and desires of guests is one way to achieve Walt Disney World's second service priority, the standard of courtesy. Toward that goal, there is a genre of processes that serve guests whose needs cannot be satisfied by existing processes, known as service attention processes.

There are two key ingredients in creating effective service attention processes. First, there must be appropriate resources to make the guest experience a good one and second, the availability of those resources must be communicated to cast and guests. Here is a closer look at how Walt Disney World extends service attention to three groups of guests who don't always fit the standard profile: international visitors, small children, and guests with disabilities.

International guests

Today's global organizations often serve an extraordinarily diverse customer base. At Walt Disney World, roughly 25 percent of guests live outside of the United States, and while all guests come to Walt Disney World to be entertained, international guests bring along a whole range of different expectations, behavioral habits, and needs. For instance, non-English-speaking guests will have trouble reading signs, to say nothing of understanding cast members and other guests.

If you visit Walt Disney World during the summer, you will often see large groups of Brazilian children, inseparable and clad in brightly colored T-shirts. Brazilians tend not to want ice in their drinks, and since gratuities are usually included on the bill in Brazil, they also tend not to tip. In Brazil, people like to tour in large groups and stay close together, often singing and chanting. As you might imagine, when a crowd of happy, boisterous children singing in Portuguese converges on a queue, it can be a disconcerting experience for other guests and cast members who are culturally predisposed to want more personal space.

To better serve Brazilian guests, Portuguese-speaking cast members are on hand to support their visits and to act as translators. There are brochures and guides in Portuguese for their use. Cast members learn about Brazilian culture and behavior. And, finally, Disney works with Brazilian tour guides to maximize their guests' experiences and break down cultural barriers. The service attention focused on Brazilian guests has been well worth the effort. They are now among Disney's top three most frequent foreign visitors.

Small children

Even though kids of all ages love Walt Disney World, the parks are not always designed to fit the needs of the smallest guests. Some attractions pack in too much excitement for small children; others contain content that isn't all that interesting to them. Guests with small children in their parties also have different concerns and needs than adult guests and older children. The recognition of these concerns led to the creation of service processes from a child's-eye view.

For instance, what can be more disappointing than standing in line at Big Thunder Mountain with your family, but not being tall enough to enter the ride? And, what do your parents do when their turn comes? Must they leave you alone or stand in line twice so each can ride the roller coaster? Instead, there is a process to answer exactly this dilemma. One parent can stay with the child while the other takes the ride. At the conclusion of the ride, the waiting parent may board immediately. And what about the child who can't ride at all? Cast members have a supply of special certificates that entitle the child to board the ride without waiting in line whenever he or she is tall enough.

Often small children do not find much to interest them in Epcot's World Showcase, so for them there is Kidcot. Kidcot includes a craft or activity in each of the national pavilions designed especially for smaller children. Every child also gets a discovery booklet that they fill out as they move from country to country. Similarly, in Downtown Disney's Marketplace, the boredom almost every small child feels when shopping is alleviated with a sticker book and set of stickers that children can collect as they move from shop to shop.

Again, service attention processes designed specifically for guests who don't fit the average profile contribute to a better experience for the guests with special needs and those in their parties.

Guests with disabilities

Every organization serves customers with disabilities and today, it is not only a moral responsibility to provide for their special needs, it is also a legal one. Several basic principles apply when designing service attention for guests with disabilities:

- Whenever possible, give guests with disabilities mainstream access to your organization. For example, at Walt Disney World, every effort is made to provide access through the main entrance of attractions. This way, guests can stay with their parties and enjoy the property along with everyone else.
- Since not all disabilities are obvious, find ways to allow guests to communicate their special needs without forcing them to explain them repeatedly. At Walt Disney World, there are three different types of Special Assistance Passes that guests can carry to communicate their needs to cast members.
- Communicate the resources available to guests with disabilities at the widest possible level. All cast members are given basic training and guidance in assisting these guests in the Traditions program. In addition, Disney University offers specialized training to managers and key cast members who have high levels of guest contact.
- Finally, communicate available resources directly to your guests. For instance, Walt Disney World offers a special guidebook detailing resources available, and one-to-one assistance at Guest Services locations.

There are a host of resources available through Walt Disney World for guests with disabilities. Among them are audio tours for those with visual disabilities. There also are wireless audio boosters, sign language performances, and reflective captioning for those with hearing disabilities. There are guest assistance packages containing scripts, flashlights, and pen and paper offered at many shows and attractions. All of these are meant to ensure that disabled guests get the best show.

All organizations have customers with needs that fall outside their standard processes. When Disney Institute client East Jefferson General Hospital examined its patient base, they found that oncology patients had very different needs and desires from maternity patients. Oncology patients wanted quiet, private waiting areas where they could meet with their families while avoiding the general population and repeated explanations of their illnesses. Maternity patients, on the other hand, wanted to celebrate their new arrivals with friends and family. In response, East Jefferson created different processes and settings for each group of patients. The hospital provides peace, quiet, and privacy outside the mainstream for oncology patients and a festive atmosphere with extra space for visitors for the maternity patients.

Before we move on, take a few minutes to identify your customers who need service attention. How can you improve their service experience?

SERVICE PROCESS DEBUGGING

In the opening of this chapter, we described the

widespread Disney trait of "plussing," that is, making an effort to continually improve the products and services offered to guests. When plussing is applied to service processes, it's known as debugging. Every service process needs to be debugged to work in the best interests of guests.

Debugging may seem at odds with the maxim of "do it right the first time," but the reality of business and life is that doing anything perfectly from the start is relatively rare. First, even though we can strive to create flawless organizations, we are dealing with living systems and they are never completely predictable. And, second, even if we could perfect our organizations, that perfection is only achieved for a short time. New technologies and techniques soon appear that allow us to make it even better.

Just ask the world's leading specialty retailer of toys, Paramus, New Jersey–based Toys "R" Us. In 1948, founder Charles Lazarus reinvented the retail toy industry, and retailing in general, when he created the first self-serve toy supermarket, a one-stop shop for everything any kid could ever want. Today's big-box specialty retail chains owe their very existence to Mr. Lazarus' business model, and Toys "R" Us is an $11.8 billion company with more than 1,500 stores and 76,000 employees.

You might think that Toys "R" Us has its business licked, but its management doesn't think that way. Times change and so do customers, and the company continues to reinvent itself and its business processes. It added a catalog sales business as the home shopping trend began to build and, with the advent of the Internet, the company started its drive to dominate toy sales in cyberspace.

In 1999, Toys "R" Us also began redesigning the guest experience in its many retail stores. The company's leaders understood that Charles Lazarus' super toy store was no longer as unique as it had been a decade before and so, they decided to up the ante in the industry once again by adding practical magic to the sales mix. After benchmarking its Quality Service at Walt Disney World and training an implementation team at Disney Institute,Toys "R" Us introduced its new brand of service. On the evening of June 13, 1999, every associate and manager in North America, including 2,000 national support staff associates, learned the basics of creating magical service experiences, delighting their guests, and a new service vision and vocabulary. At midnight on June 14, the "magic moment" struck and every employee knew that making practical magic for their guests was Toys "R" Us' new business.

Like Toys "R" Us, you can recognize the realities of an ever-changing marketplace and continually improve your business model and processes or you can insist that you got it right the first time and stick your head in the sand. If you chose the first option, read on. If not, listen to Michael Eisner: "Standing still is not an option. Either you take calculated risks to grow or you slowly wither and die."[8] In other words, there is no real choice. You still need to read on.

Opportunities for the improvement of service processes tend to arise from two kinds of circumstances.

The first grow out of design flaws or oversights or the availability of improved technologies. We, as service organizations, own those problems. The second emerge directly out of the needs of guests, or guest-owned actions. Let's take a closer look at these kinds of improvement opportunities.

Debugging flawed processes

One of the most popular features at the Disney theme parks is the ability to meet and be photographed with Mickey Mouse and the entire cast of Disney characters. Character appearances have been a standard part of the guest experience since 1955 when Disneyland first opened. For guests, however, spending the time they want with the characters has not always been a simple task.

When guestology studies revealed the desire for greater access to character appearances and the difficulty of navigating the crowds that quickly formed around the characters, the experience began to be debugged. First came Toontown, which brought the characters into one area that could be managed for the best guest experience. Then fixed character greeting locations were established throughout the parks and their locations were communicated in guidebooks and with signage. And, finally, to ensure that guests could find Pocahontas or Snow White or another favorite character, CHiP was created. CHiP is the Character Hotline and Information Program, which is a telephone number that every cast member can call to tell guests exactly when and where to find each character, wherever they might be.

Sometimes debugging a process flaw requires inconveniencing a customer, such as when a product must be recalled. As anyone who has witnessed the public relations nightmares that ensue when these incidents are mishandled knows, they can be very damaging to an organization's reputation and its bottom line. On the other hand, a well-conducted debugging can enhance both customer loyalty and long-term profits.

The Volkswagen Group experienced the latter phenomenon soon after the launch of its popular New Beetle in 1998. The company had undertaken the most elaborate launch in its history to celebrate the rebirth of its classic VW Bug. To introduce the new car to its dealers, the company brought 9,000 employees and family members from its North American headquarters and its dealership network to Walt Disney World for seminars and some fun. The consumer launch was even more extensive, featuring marketing and advertising campaigns that blanketed North America.

After a hugely successful launch that had car buyers signing up on waiting lists for the New Beetle, the company discovered there was a chance that a wiring assembly in some of the cars could have been installed in a way that might lead to chafing. The company was concerned that, in the worst case, this had the potential to cause a fire. In a textbook example of service debugging, the company authorized a full recall. No customer would ever have to wonder if his or her new car was safe. To compensate their customers for the inconvenience of having to return their new cars to the dealer for repair, Volkswagen authorized a $100 allowance per customer. To apologize, dealers were authorized to spend the money any way the customer wanted.

The company's fast, sensitive response saved the day. Not only did its customer satisfaction numbers remain constant, the company actually received thank-you letters from New Beetle owners. The car, which had been targeted to eventually build to annual sales of 50,000 vehicles, sold more than 70,000 units in its first year and continues to sell between 70,000 and 80,000 units per year.

Improving outdated processes

The ticketing system at Walt Disney World is a good example of a debugging opportunity that arose from changes in technology. The ticketing process had grown extremely complicated over the decades. Cast members spent more time worrying about tickets than serving guests. There were 2,000 active categories of paper tickets to manage and ticket changes required at least a three-week lead time. On top of that the printed tickets were useable prior to their issuance, so there were many loss control and security issues inherent in the system.

The rapid development of automated networks and smart card technology allowed Walt Disney World to completely reengineer the process. A new Automated Ticketing System (ATS) based on magnetically coded, credit card-sized tickets was put into place. Now, there are only eight categories of tickets that can be encoded in an infinite number of variations, and tickets are not "live" until the point of sale. Even better, the encoded card is simply swiped at the automated turnstiles located at the entrance to the parks, leaving the cast plenty of time to greet and assist guests.

Debugging guest-owned processes

Guests sometimes make mistakes. If they are abandoned to deal with the results of those problems alone, we are abrogating our responsibility to create Quality Service experiences. Providing a magical guest experience means solving the problems guests create with the same dedication with which we attack the service problems that we create on our own. Chapter 1 described the debugging effort that Walt Disney World cast members created to help guests who had forgotten where they had parked their cars. That is a perfect example of a process improvement designed in response to a guest-owned debugging project.

Sometimes the guest-owned problem is very minor indeed. They might have a squeaky wheel on a baby stroller or pop a button, or, as anyone with poor vision well knows, lose one of those tiny, impossible-to-find screws that hold a pair of eyeglasses together. Enter Walt Disney World's Magic Pouch. The security cast members at Epcot invented the Magic Pouch in response to the minor problems that guests commonly encounter. Each now wears a pouch containing the solutions to those common problems: a can of lubricating oil, a sewing kit and safety pins, and even an eyeglasses repair kit. *Voilà*, problem solved and guest experience enhanced.

Our examination of the major elements of Quality Service Cycle is complete. We've explored how to center efforts on guests and discover what they want, how to create a service theme and standards, and the three major service delivery systems all companies share: cast, setting, and process. There is one task left, the most important of all: putting them together to create the practical magic of Quality Service.

End Notes

[1] See Bob Thomas's *Walt Disney: An American Original* (Hyperion, 1994) for a full account of the early years.

[2] The quote appears on p. 185 of *The Illusion of Life: Disney Animation* by Frank Thomas and Ollie Johnston (Hyperion, 1995). The book contains a detailed examination of the Disney animation process by two men who experienced it firsthand.

[3] The quote appears on p. 102 of Richard Schickel's *The Disney Version* (Ivan R. Dee, 1997).

[4] Walt Disney's quote appears on p. 244 of Bob Thomas's *Walt Disney* (Hyperion, 1994).

[5] *Ibid.*, p. 290.

[6] See p. 240–248 in Michael Eisner's *Work In Progress* (Hyperion, 1999) for a fuller description of the founding of The Disney Store retail chain. The quote appears on p. 244.

[7] See p. 272–273 of Bob Thomas' *Walt Disney* (Hyperion, 1994) for a fuller description of Disneyland's opening day.

[8] The quote appears on p. 233 of Michael Eisner's *Work In Progress* (Hyperion, 1999).

Quality Service Cues

Take a process orientation to service delivery. Roughly three-quarters of service is delivered via processes. Processes are the policies, tasks, and procedures used to deliver service.

Collect and analyze combustion statements. Combustion statements are indicators of service issues that need to be solved. Listen to and study your guests to identify and optimize those issues before combustion points become explosion points.

Optimize guest flow throughout the service experience. Create the perfect service flow by optimizing the operation of products and services, allowing guests to self-manage their experience, and effectively managing unavoidable waits.

Equip your cast to communicate with guests. Fielding questions immediately is an important component of customer satisfaction. Provide your cast with the right information in the right manner at the right time.

Create processes for guests who need service attention. Treat all of your guests like VIPs—very important, very individual people. Identify guests who need service attention, such as children, international customers, and people with disabilities, implement processes designed to ensure they get a positive service experience, and communicate those processes throughout the organization.

Debug service processes continuously. "Plus" your service processes at every opportunity. Fix design flaws and oversights, adapt new technologies and techniques, and solve your customers' problems before they ask for help.

CHAPTER 6

THE MAGIC OF INTEGRATION

By the early 1940s, there was no dispute over the fact that The Walt Disney Company had become the world's leading animation studio. The staff of the studio, the facilities and equipment they had to work with, and the filmmaking process itself had combined to create the greatest animated entertainment audiences had ever seen. Walt Disney had harnessed the magic of integration and, in doing so, had turned out great films, such as the animation classic *Snow White*, which earned a spot as the highest grossing film of all time until it was finally surpassed by *Gone with the Wind*.

Whether by plan or intuition, Walt had built the capabilities of the three delivery systems that all organizations share. His cast, the studio staff, was the best in the world. Thanks to the extensive in-house training and apprenticeship programs described in the opening of chapter 3, the company was continually building the competence and expertise of its workforce. Walt was also busy creating a world-class setting for the production of animated films. In 1940, the company began moving into its brand-new studio in Burbank, which Walt had built with his usual attention to detail. And, finally, as described in the opening of the last chapter, step by step and innovation by innovation, Walt had created a production process capable of managing and making a full-length animation feature.

When Walt brought these three delivery systems together, his dream of turning animation into a respected form of entertainment was fully realized. "All the Hollywood brass turned out for my cartoon!" he remembered long after the triumphant opening of *Snow White*. "That was the thing. And it went way back to when I first came out here and I went to my first premiere. I'd never seen one in my life. I saw all these Hollywood celebrities comin' in and I just had a funny feeling. I just hoped that some day they'd be going to a premiere of a cartoon. Because people would depreciate the cartoon. You know, they'd kind of look down."[1]

Walt put the three delivery systems of Quality Service together once again to create the unique entertainment known as Disneyland. He staffed his new kind of amusement park with a new kind of employee. Hucksters and the sour-faced need not apply. Instead, Walt insisted on a clean-cut image and a permanent smile. And, he established the first corporate university to teach his cast how to treat Disneyland's guests. The setting was planned, constructed, and plussed down to the smallest detail. And, as we saw in chapter 5, processes, such as the timing of the Jungle Boat cruise, were refined and executed down to the second.

The result, not counting Black Sunday, that rough opening day when the crowds simply overran the new park, was a resounding success. Within seven weeks of opening, 1 million guests had visited Disneyland. The attendance exceeded the company's targeted goals by 50 percent, and guests were spending 30 percent more than anticipated. In 1950, the Disney Company had revenues of $5 million. In 1955, when Disneyland opened, revenues were $27 million. And, by year-end 1959, the company's revenues had grown to $70 million. The magic of integration had turned Walt Disney's cartoon studio into an entertainment empire.[2]

Integration is still working its magic throughout The Walt Disney Company today. Every moviegoer who sat entranced through *Toy Story, The Lion King,* or a slew of other Disney hits was treated to an integrated dose of Quality Service. Every one of the millions of annual visitors to Disneyland, Walt Disney World, Disneyland Paris, and Tokyo Disneyland get the same integrated guest experience, even though they would surely not describe their vacations in exactly those terms.

PUTTING QUALITY SERVICE TOGETHER

Here's one scene you will never witness: Your neighbors have just returned home after a vacation at Walt Disney World. "How did it go?" you ask. "Wow," say the parents, "you've gotta experience that Walt Disney World service theme to believe it. Those folks know their service standards."

"Yeah," chime in the kids, "that Grand Floridian, boy, talk about a performance culture. And, you have to see how they combine cast, setting, and process in The

Twilight Zone Tower of Terror to deliver Quality Service!"

Guests are surrounded by all of those things, but concepts like service standards and delivery systems are the infrastructure of the Quality Service Cycle and, like many infrastructures, this one is transparent to the customer. Like a surfer on the Internet who effortlessly jumps from site to site navigating around the globe with a click of the mouse, guests can see and judge the service the infrastructure delivers. So, when your neighbors start raving about their experiences staying at the Grand Floridian or dropping down the The Twilight Zone Tower of Terror, what they are really describing is how well all of the elements of the Quality Service Cycle have been integrated to deliver a seamless, magical guest experience.

Integration is the operative word. Integration is the process of bringing all of the elements of Quality Service together to create a complete experience. It is the critical, final step of the Quality Service Cycle. Quality Service is defined as paying attention to details and exceeding expectations. Integration helps identify which details to attend to and what expectations to exceed.

When the elements of a system are properly integrated, a booster rocket for progress is the result. The value of the whole organization becomes greater than the sum of its parts. This multiplier effect happens because the effective operation of one system not only achieves its own goals, it also supports and enhances the goals of other systems. For instance, the Whispering Canyon Café in Wilderness Lodge opens onto the main lobby and its cast is costumed and acts like characters from the Old West. As a result, the cast does more than simply serve meals to guests. They entertain the people in the restaurant with their colorful actions and accents, and they add to the show of the entire main lobby. The cast is adding value to the setting.

But the elements of a system must be *properly* integrated. It is possible to make one element more effective at the cost of another. The cars at the Haunted Mansion could be faster and more guests would see the show each hour. The guest flow process would be more efficient, but what effect would that have on the cast, not to mention the ability of guests to enjoy the details of the setting? Elements in a system must be aligned to work together or they might detract from each other.

Exactly what is integrated and aligned to create Quality Service? The simple answer is, the service standards of the organization and its primary delivery systems. The service standards—at Walt Disney World, safety, courtesy, show, and efficiency—represent behaviors that allow the service theme to be fulfilled, and the delivery systems, cast, setting, and process, are the distribution channels used to ensure those standards reach guests. So, the goal of integration is the delivery of your organization's service standards to your guests via cast, process, and setting.

Every service standard can be distributed over all three delivery systems. At Walt Disney World, safety is delivered through the cast, setting, and processes. The cast is trained at the organizational and departmental levels in safety techniques. The setting delivers safety, too. One-half of the boardwalk at the BoardWalk Resort is supported by steel; it was designed as a fire lane and provides emergency access to the stores and restaurants lining the vintage Atlantic City oceanfront. And, finally, safety is built into processes, such as the designed-in ability to slow and stop attractions when loading and unloading guests. The standards of courtesy, show, and efficiency can also be distributed over all three delivery systems.

Even though all three delivery systems can distribute each service standard, there are certain delivery systems that are especially well aligned with specific standards. At the Disney Institute, these are known as headliners, because of the power inherent in these special combinations. For instance, although courtesy is delivered via setting and process, it is the cast that is especially suited to deliver the personal touch to the guests. Likewise, the Walt Disney World standard of show is best communicated via setting, and efficiency is often a process-related issue. Headliners will vary depending on your organization's service standards, but you should identify them and make sure that they are addressed during the integration phase of Quality Service development.

That there are natural integration headliners doesn't mean other delivery systems can be ignored. As stated, all three delivery systems should be used to distribute service standards. The secondary systems are called landmarks, because they offer fine opportunities to exceed guest expectations. It is important that a process delivers an efficient service experience, but many of us expect streamlined, timesaving transactions these days. When the cast and the layout of the organization streamline that experience even more, however, customers are often wowed.

THE INTEGRATION MATRIX

The Integration Matrix will help guide you through the process of Quality Service analysis and improvement. The matrix in the diagram below is a simple chart designed to track the distribution of service standards through delivery systems. To build one of your own, create an expanded tic-tac-toe board with enough rows along the side to list your organization's service standards and three columns across the top to accommodate the delivery systems of cast, setting, and process. Now, insert your service standards on the side in order of priority from top to bottom. (Remember to prioritize the service standards.)

Integration Matrix

	Cast	Setting	Process
Safety			
Courtesy			
Show			
Efficiency			

Take a moment to consider the empty boxes in the body of the matrix. Each one of them represents an intersection between a single service standard and a discrete delivery system. In the first box in the upper left-hand corner of the diagram, safety and cast are combined. In the last box in the lower right-hand corner, efficiency and process meet. Each of these meetings represents a service moment of truth, a point at which you can affect the quality of the guest experience. Each box asks the user a question. For example, in that upper left hand corner, it asks: How will your cast deliver safety to guests? In the lower right: How will your processes create a more efficient guest experience? By filling in the answers in each box, you can create a complete Quality Service experience.

The ability to design a fresh, new integrated approach to the guest experience is just one of the uses of the matrix. It can also be used as a diagnostic tool to isolate, analyze, and brainstorm solutions to service lapses. You can fine-tune the matrix by imposing other parameters. For example, you could use it to identify effective *and* inexpensive approaches to creating service moments. And, finally, the Integration Matrix is a useful benchmarking tool. It can be used to analyze a competitor's service or a partner's.

The level at which you can apply the matrix is similarly diverse. It can be used at the strategic level. For example, you might generate broad boundaries for Quality Service by using it to analyze and improve the end-to-end guest experience. You could also narrow the focus of the matrix to the departmental or single process level by aiming it at sales, customer service, or collections. Or, you can narrow the focus of the matrix even further by honing in on and expanding a single service moment, in essence, concentrating on one box in the matrix. By adjusting the focus of the matrix, it becomes useful at all levels of the organization from the senior leadership team to a group of frontline cast members who are charged with creating incremental improvements in their own show. Here is a look at the specific Integration Matrix from the Disney Vacation Club.

INTEGRATING SERVICE AT DISNEY VACATION CLUB

Launched with the opening of the Disney Vacation Club Resort (now Disney's Old Key West Resort) in October 1991, Disney Vacation Club (DVC) was created in response to guests' desire to own a piece of the magic. This collection of shared resorts, is a pioneering concept that Disney calls "vacation ownership."

DVC worked hard to transcend the limited flexibility that is typical of timeshares. For instance, Vacation Club members enjoy a point system that allows them maximum flexibility when using their vacation time. In addition to using the points to visit any Disney Resort worldwide as well as myriad other destinations, members can use the points by the room night, for different accommodations based on their needs at that specific time, and at any time of the year.

It proved to be an immensely popular program and

guest demand led to fast expansion. Old Key West Resort was joined by Disney's Vero Beach Resort, the first resort ever built away from the theme parks. Soon thereafter, Disney's Hilton Head Island Resort opened. The number of resorts on property also expanded. In addition to Old Key West Resort, Vacation Club members can now choose to stay at Disney's BoardWalk Villas, Disney's Wilderness Lodge or, starting in 2002, the Villas at Disney's Beach Club Resort.

DVC also worked hard to transcend the somewhat tarnished reputation of timeshare sales. Although there are plenty of high-quality property developers and operators in the industry, the word "timeshare" can conjure up an unsavory image in the public imagination. To create a shared ownership program that could exist in harmony with and support the Disney service theme, DVC needed to reinvent the sales experience to fit the Walt Disney World service standards. Here's how the Integration Matrix can be used to analyze that effort.

	Cast	Setting	Process
Safety	Training in property-wide and DVC safety techniques and policy	First response features; safe materials; emergency access	Traffic flow; cast response; evacuation plans

The first questions, of course, involve DVC's top service priority, the nonnegotiable standard of safety. How does DVC ensure guest and cast safety? Happily, the answers to those questions are already well established at Walt Disney World. The sales cast delivers a safe experience by being prepared for emergencies. They get the same property-wide and location-specific training that all Walt Disney World cast members receive. The setting features fire extinguishers and emergency first-aid equipment. It offers access to emergency services vehicles and is built from materials that enhance guest security. Processes were created to ensure consistent and quick cast response to emergencies. Traffic flow and evacuation patterns were established.

By simply moving down to the next row on the Integration Matrix, we receive our next series of questions. This time, they cover the delivery of the standard of courtesy in the preview experience. Since the delivery system of cast is the headliner for courtesy, DVC ensured that the cast plays a primary role in delivering a courteous sales experience. The company went against the stereotype of the timeshare industry and focused on developing long-term relationships with club members. It makes sure that the DVC sales cast believes in the value offered in club membership and emphasizes helping guests over selling them. DVC also brought all of the Walt Disney World Performance Tips to bear on cast behavior.

With actions of the headliner established, we can start thinking about how the landmark delivery systems extend the standard of courtesy. At DVC, they built care and courtesy into the setting. For example, there is a fully stocked umbrella stand at the preview center so that no guest ever gets soaked during a tour. And, since guests often bring their entire family, there is a supervised child-care facility in the center, so that parents can concentrate on the presentation and children don't get bored. The sales process was also designed to ensure courteous treatment. The DVC sales cast never "double teams" a guest or otherwise attempts to force a purchase.

Moving another row down the Integration Matrix, we are confronted with a third set of questions. This time, we consider the service standard of show and how it is distributed by DVC's cast, setting, and process. Starting with the headliner, in this case, setting, DVC decided that each preview center needed to reflect a "welcome home" atmosphere. Quality and detailing are hallmarks of each center's construction. The preview center at Disney's BoardWalk Villas, for example, captures the excitement, color, and whimsy of a mid-Atlantic boardwalk from the 1920s.

	Cast	Setting	Process
Courtesy	Build long-term relationships; be passionate about product; use Performance Tips	Umbrellas for guests; supervised playroom for children	One sales cast member per guest; no hard-sell techniques

To further communicate show, DVC extended it into the landmark systems of cast and process. The cast received training from a performance consultant, who showed them how to keep each new performance fresh and interesting for guests, no matter how often they had to repeat it each day. Whether they buy a membership or not, DVC ensures that guests literally leave with a good taste in their mouths by treating them to boardwalk-style fare such as cotton candy and salt water taffy. "I think what [guests are] pleasantly surprised to find," says a

DVC marketing manager, "is one of the toughest deci-sions that they have to make at the end of the sales process is whether to have cotton candy or taffy."[3]

	Cast	Setting	Process
Show	Sales as an onstage performance; performance training	Your home away from home; interior design; themed treats	Leave with a good taste in your mouth; sweets as a last step

The final row in the analysis of DVC's effort to build a preview experience that embodies the Walt Disney World service theme and standards asks questions about the stan-dard of efficiency. The headliner here is the delivery system of process, and one way that DVC ensures that the sales process is an efficient one is by bringing a quality assur-ance cast member into the process whenever a guest decides to buy a membership. The QA cast member sits down with the guest and goes over all of the paperwork and contracts that the guest will sign. In this way, DVC ensures that every guest fully understands the commitment and cost and that no guest ever leaves confused or feeling pressured into a purchase.

In what should start feeling like a familiar pattern by now, DVC then considered the landmark systems of cast and setting and how they could deliver an efficient preview experience. The cast, for example, was taught to tell guests the important details about club membership up front. They explain the product, quote the cost of membership, and give the guest a time estimate for the preview process immediately. In this way, DVC does not waste the guest's or the cast member's time. Finally, the setting of the Commodore House is designed to facilitate the flow of guests through the preview process. From a greeting in the entrance lobby, each guest is escorted into a themed presentation room where the sales cast presents the benefits of membership. An adjoining storybook room features architectural models of different DVC resorts. A physical tour of a real model home and resort property follows and then the guest is escorted back to the preview center and parlor, a room where they have some private, quiet space to discuss a purchase and make unhurried decisions.

	Cast	Setting	Process
Efficiency	Provide critical purchase information up front	Setting supports efficient guest flow; quiet, private room for closing	Quality assurance team member at commitment

That completes the DVC Integration Matrix, but there are a couple of codicils worth noting before we put it all together. First, to keep this case study manageable, we described only a few of the ideas in use at DVC in each service moment. In fact, each box has a long list of actions designed to deliver a magical service experience. Second, for clarity, we described the use of the matrix in a linear fashion. In reality, you can start anywhere and proceed as convenient. The important thing is that in the end every box has been thoroughly considered. With that in mind, here's what DVC's completed Integration Matrix looks like:

Disney Vacation Club's Integration Matrix

	Cast	Setting	Process
Safety	Training in property-wide and DVC safety techniques and policies	First response features; safe materials; emergency access	Traffic flow; cast response; evacuation plans
Courtesy	Build long-term relationships; be passionate about product; use Performance Tips	Umbrellas for guests; supervised playroom for children	One sales cast member per guest; no hard-sell techniques
Show	Sales as an onstage performance; performance training	Your home away from home; interior design; themed treats	Leave with a good taste in your mouth; sweets as last step
Efficiency	Provide critical purchase information up front	Setting supports efficient guest flow; quiet, private room for closing	Quality assurance team member at commitment

THREE ELEMENTS OF MAGICAL SERVICE MOMENTS

Bill Martin, one of the original Imagineers who helped design Disneyland, made the following observation about his experiences working with Walt Disney. "Walt used to say, 'I don't care what you can't do. I want to hear what you *can* do.' If there were fifteen ways to solve a problem, Walt was looking for all fifteen."[4] That is one reason why Walt would have liked the Integration Matrix.

One of the best features of the Integration Matrix is that it leaves room for more than one right answer to creating a great service moment. As you begin to use the Integration Matrix to develop service features, each intersection of service standard and delivery system will yield numerous alternatives. You may choose to implement one idea or all of them or any number in between.

When the time comes to analyze all of the ideas you have generated using the Integration Matrix and you begin deciding which ideas to implement, there are three features of great service moments to keep in mind. They are high-touch, high-show, and high-tech.

High-touch refers to the need to build interaction into the guest experience. For the most part, we humans enjoy connecting with each other. So, if we create service solutions that give guests a chance to participate, make choices, and interact with the cast, they will connect more intimately with the experience and the organization that is providing it. High-touch is a quality that cast is particularly adept at providing.

At Walt Disney World, when you see a cast member taking a family picture for a guest, you are witnessing a service that offers high-touch. When you call the WDW-DINE line (407-939-3463), to make a priority seating at a restaurant, you are seeing high-touch applied to a process. And, when you enter the giant-size, soft-surface playground that is the *Honey, I Shrunk the Kids* Movie Set Adventure, you are getting high-touch from a setting.

High-show refers to the need to build vivid presentations into the guest experience. When we choose service solutions that are high-show, guests enjoy colorful, memorable experiences—the kind that they will talk about to others for months and perhaps years to come. High-show is a quality that is closely aligned to the delivery system of setting, so be sure to think about how to build it into designs for your organization's physical assets.

Disney's Grand Floridian Resort & Spa is a good example of a high-show setting. Patterned after the grand hotels of the late 1800s, it is a 900-room trip back to the Victorian Era, and every detail supports the show. You can see high-show in a process at Epcot's IllumiNations program. Every night, fireworks, lasers, fountains, and music are combined to create a spectacular wrap-up to a day at the park. And, visit Disney–MGM Studios for a look at how cast can deliver high-show. There, the Streetmosphere performers are costumed and perform as the characters you would likely encounter in the streets of mythic Hollywood. Starlets and taxi drivers, and even autograph hounds, entertain guests as they move through the park.

High-tech refers to the need to build speed, accuracy, and expertise into service solutions. When we do a good job of creating high-tech service, we give guests the gift of time, build products and services that approach the cutting edge of the possible, and often, maximize our own profits. Processes are particularly well suited to deliver high-tech, so as you create and improve processes, think about how they can be made more efficient and entertaining with technology.

Walt Disney World's new automated ticketing system described in the last chapter is a process that encompasses the feature of high-tech. To see high-tech in a setting, take a spin on the Disney–MGM Studio's Rock 'N Roller Coaster starring Aerosmith. The vehicles accelerate from 0 to 60 miles per hour in 2.8 seconds, exert 5gs of pressure on the rider, and with five speakers per seat, it sounds as if the rock band came along for the ride.

And finally, to see high-tech at work in the delivery system of cast, take a behind-the-scenes look at Reedy Creek Emergency Services. The paramedics and firefighters employ many high-tech solutions to protect the cast members and guests of Walt Disney World. To get a feel for what that means, consider that since the property opened in 1971, there has been less than $200,000 in structural fire loss. A single house fire can easily exceed that figure.

High-touch, high-show, and high-tech. As you explore the ways to make the most of your service moments, be sure to keep all three features in mind.

ONE FINAL TOOL:
THE STORYBOARD

There is one more effective technique for the Quality Service Cycle tool kit—storyboarding. The storyboard is an effective way to map out a service solution and to build a plan for its implementation. Storyboarding is used throughout The Walt Disney Company and it is a familiar technique in the motion picture industry, too. But, what many of those who use it don't know is that it originated in the Disney animation studios back in the 1930s.

According to Walt, the storyboard was invented by Webb Smith, an animator and one of the first storymen at the studio. When Webb planned a story, he would draw it instead of describing the action in words. At first, he simply spread the drawings out over the floor of his office, but soon he graduated to pinning them in order onto the walls. In this way, the unfolding story gained a valuable visual dimension. According to legend, Walt was none too happy with the innovation. He had just redecorated the offices and the marred walls in Webb's office stuck out like a sore thumb. But Walt also recognized the order imposed by the posted drawings and the ease with which the entire feature could be analyzed and manipulated. So he ordered four-foot by eight-foot corkboards and the storyboard was born.[5]

Soon, every Disney cartoon first saw life on a storyboard, and the boards themselves moved to new departments as the project progressed. The storymen would pitch their ideas to Walt on a storyboard, color and sound were both added using the storyboard as reference point, etc. When Walt hijacked the studio's animators to design the attractions for Disneyland, they brought the storyboard along with them. And, today, it has evolved into a ubiquitous technique among the Imagineers. Here's how they describe its use:

> The first step in developing a three-dimensional world is to see it in two-dimensional storyboards. . . . For each ride, show, or attraction, a logical story sequence is created. Almost every aspect of the project is broken down into progressive scene sketches, called storyboard panels, that reflect the beginning, middle, and end of our guest's park experience.
>
> The boards are eventually covered with every written thought, idea, and rough sketch we can come up with. If need be, a separate set of storyboards is developed for the sole purpose of establishing the camera shots required for the videos or film that may be part of the attraction. As they are fine-tuned, the boards are used as a presentation tool to sell the idea to management, and to explain the concept to all of the Imagineering departments that will contribute to the evolution of the project.
>
> A completed storyboard offers us the first chance to experience a new ride or show and see how the idea might—or might not—work."[6]

As might already be obvious, the storyboard is also an effective way to visualize and organize the development of the service solutions generated by the Integration Matrix. It offers a way to map the experience from a guest's perspective and improve and troubleshoot the proposed action before it ever gets off the, well, storyboard.

Here are two fast guidelines for storyboarding: 1) For the non-artists among us, don't be intimidated by the use of drawings. At Disney, there are plenty of great artists, but storyboarding is not about the beauty of the drawings. It is about the ability to see and consider ideas through your guests' eyes. 2) Don't restrict the storyboard to drawings. Pin up fabric swatches, color samples, photos, text, brainstorming ideas, and anything else that helps communicate a better image of the intended project. Any one of these items might trigger a breakthrough that will take the level of your service another notch higher.

That is how the elements of Quality Service come together at Walt Disney World. The service theme generates standards. The standards are defined and delivered using three basic systems that every organization shares: its people, its physical assets, and its processes. And, finally, all three are integrated and aligned. That is the business behind the Disney brand of magic. Put it to work in your organization, and soon you will be creating some practical magic of your own.

You have completed a full revolution around the Quality Service Cycle. We've pulled back the curtain and shown you how the level of Quality Service that has made Walt Disney World a world-class benchmark is created. And, with the generous permission and assistance of a select group of Disney Institute clients, you have seen how organizations in business, education, healthcare, and government have applied the elements of the Quality Service Cycle to improve their own guests' experiences.

Endnotes

[1] Walt Disney's quote appears in Bob Thomas' *Walt Disney: An American Original* (Hyperion, 1994), p. 141.

[2] *Ibid.,* p. 285.

[3] The quote is from a videotaped interview with DVC cast members conducted by the Disney Institute.

[4] Bill Martin's quote appears on p. 102 of Amy Boothe Green and Howard Green's *Remembering Walt: Favorite Memories of Walt Disney* (Disney Editions, 1999).

[5] The genesis of storyboarding is related on p. 147 and 148 of Richard Schickel's *The Disney Version* (Ivan R. Dee, 1997).

[6] The quoted material appears on p. 40 of *Walt Disney Imagineering* (Hyperion, 1996). Read the book for an in-depth look at the design-and-build process used by the Disney Imagineers.

Quality Service Cues

Build a service organization greater than the sum of its parts with integration. Integration is the work of aligning and distributing your service standards over the three delivery systems of cast, setting, and process.

Meet guest expectations with headliners; exceed guest expectations with landmarks. Headliners are those combinations of standards and delivery systems that are natural matches. At Walt Disney World, they are cast and courtesy, setting and show, and process and efficiency. Landmarks are the remaining combinations. They can be used to distribute service standards in unexpected ways to surprise and delight guests.

Make the Integration Matrix part of your organizational toolbox. The Integration Matrix is an expanded tic-tac-toe board that combines service standards and delivery systems. Use it to analyze and manage the design and development of Quality Service.

Manage every service moment of truth. On the Integration Matrix, each combination of a service standard and a delivery system represents a service moment of truth. Each should be fully considered and developed to deliver a magical service moment.

Choose service solutions that are high-touch, high-show, and high-tech. When analyzing service solutions, look for those that meet a guest's need for interaction, vivid presentation, and efficiency.

Plan and manage solution implementations using storyboards. Use storyboards, visual maps of service solutions, as an aid to implementation.

INDEX

P.O. Box 10093
Lake Buena Vista, FL 32830-0093
Phone: (407) 566-2633
Fax: (407) 566-7685
Web site: disneyinstitute.com